S0-GGO-747

FROM "SUPERMAN" TO MAN

" 'Pardon's the word to all.' Whatever folly men commit, be their shortcomings or their vices what they may, let us exercise forbearance: remembering that when these faults appear in others:it is our follies and vices that we behold. They are the shortcomings of humanity, to which we belong; whose faults, one and all, we share; yes, even those very faults at which we now wax so very indignant, merely because they have not yet appeared in ourselves. They are faults that do not lie on the surface. But they exist down there in the depths of our nature; and should anything call them forth, they will come and show themselves, just as we now see them in others. One man, it is true, may have faults that are absent in his fellow; and it is undeniable that the sum total of bad qualities is in some cases very large; for the difference of individuality between man and man passes all measure."—Schopenhauer.

FROM "SUPERMAN" TO MAN

FIRST DAY

"A moral, sensible and well-bred man
Will not affront me; and no other can."

—Cowper.

The limited was speeding on to California over the snow-blanketed prairies of Iowa. On car "Bulwer" the passengers had all gone to bed, and Dixon, the porter, his duties finished sought the more comfortable warmth of the smoker, a book—Finot's "Race Prejudice"—under his arm.

Settling himself in a corner of the long leather couch, he opened the book in search of the place he had been reading last. It was where the author spoke of the Germans and their doctrine of the racial inferiority of the remainder of the white race.

Finding it, he began to read, "The notion of superior and inferior peoples spread like wild-fire through Germany. German literature, philosophy, and politics were profoundly influenced by it. . . ." Then he looked up. A passenger, fully dressed, had rushed into the room.

"Is this Boone we are coming into, porter?" he demanded excitedly in a foreign accent, at the same time peering anxiously out of the window at the twinkling lights of the town toward which the train was rushing.

"No, sir," reassured Dixon, "we'll not be in Boone for twenty minutes yet. This is Ames."

"Thank you," said the passenger, relieved, "the porter on my car has gone to bed, and I feared I would be carried by." He started to leave but turned when half-way and asked. "May I ride here with you and get off when we get there?"

"Certainly, sir," welcomed Dixon, cordially, "make yourself at home. Where are your grips?" and dropping his book on the seat, Dixon went for his bags.

Returning with them, he placed them in a corner. The passenger was reading the book.

FROM "SUPERMAN" TO MAN

"Thank you," said the passenger. Holding out the book, he said, "I took the liberty to look at this, and I find it's an old favorite of mine."

"Ah, is it? exclaimed Dixon with heightened cordiality.

"This is the first English translation I have seen," continued the passenger, "and I think it pretty good."

"Yes, sir, very good. But I prefer it in the original."

"In the original! Vous parlez francais, alors?"

"Mais oui, Monsieur."

"Where did you learn French,—in New Orleans?"

"I began it in college and learnt it in France," replied Dixon, in the same language.

"You have been in France! What part?"

"Bordeaux."

"Bordeaux? How long?"

"Two years and a half."

"Studying?"

"No, sir. I was Spanish correspondent for Simon and Co., wine merchants."

"You speak Spanish, too, eh? What are you, Cuban?"

"No, American, but I have been to Cuba. I learned Spanish in the Philippines."

"You travelled a great deal.

"Yes. It's just my luck. I returned from the Philippines in time to get a job as valet to a gentleman about to tour South South America, becoming six months later his private secretary. Together we visited the principal countries of the world. Mr. Simpson died while we were in Bordeaux. That accounts for my stay there."

"Didn't you like it in France?"

"Oh, I liked it better than anywhere on earth, but along came the world war and I joined up with the American forces. After the war, with my job gone, I came back with the boys to America. And here I am."

"I think with your knowledge of French and Spanish you ought to be able to get a better job than this."

"Well, I have never been able to. And when one has a family he must get the wherewithal to live some way."

"But have you tried to get something better?"

FROM "SUPERMAN" TO MAN

"I am trying continually. On my return from Europe I advertised for a job as French and Spanish correspondent. I received many replies, but when the employers saw me, they made various excuses. One, declaring he was broadminded, would have but me, but his offer was so small that I refused it on principle."

"Too bad. You said you went to college? Do you mind coming a little closer. I can't hear for the noise."

Dixon came nearer. "I spent a semester and a half at Yale," he said. "Then came the chance to travel that I spoke of."

The conversation drifted to railroad life. The passenger told Dixon about a clash between the porter on his car and a fussy passenger that afternoon. "Do you often meet people like that," he asked.

"No, sir. Nearly everyone I meet on the road is very pleasant. I am sure that if that wise old Greek who said, "Most men are bad!" had gained his knowledge of human nature on a sleeping car his verdict would have been altogether different. I never knew before that there were so many kind, agreeable persons until I had this position. One meets a grouchy person at such rare intervals that he can afford to be liberal then. I can recall an incident similar to the one you have just told me. Would you care to hear it?"

"Certainly."

"One day while waiting on a drawing-room passenger I made a mistake. This man, who had got on the train with a grouch, having previously wrangled with the train- and the sleeping-car conductors, at once began to abuse me vociferously in spite of my earnest apology. I took it all calmly, at the same time racking my mind for some polite, but effective retort. As I noted the ludicrousness of his ruffled features an inspiration came to me, whereby I could bring his conduct effectively to his notice. In the room was a full-length mirror, made into the state-room door. Swinging this door around I brought it right in front of him, where he could get a full view of his distorted features, at the same time saying with good nature, 'See, sir, the mirror does you a strange injustice today.' The ridicule was too much for him. He stopped immediately, then started to explode again,

FROM "SUPERMAN" TO MAN

and, apparently at a loss for words, sat down. He later proved
to be one of the finest passengers I have ever served."

The subject of the book came up again, "I remember the great
stir it created when it appeared," said the passenger. "Finot
has rendered a great service to humanity. He well deserves
the honor conferred on him—Officer of the Legion of Honor."

"Yes. He has been rightly called one of the makers of modern
France," said Dixon. "Is it true that he is Polish, sir?"

"Yes. He was born in Poland."

Outside were the twinkling lights of a town. "Ah, here we
are coming into Boone now," said Dixon.

"Good-by," said the passenger, genuine regret in his voice,
"I'm sorry our acquaintance is so short. I'm stopping here only
for the night and will go on to Los Angeles tomorrow. I'd
like to have had you all the way."

"I'm sure you'll have a pleasant porter tomorrow," said
Dixon, cheerily, grasping the other's proffered hand.

Dixon turned to receive the new-coming passengers. He
helped them inside, saw them to bed, and returned to the smoker
to read his book. But too tired to concentrate his thoughts on
the scientific matter, he closed the volume, placed it behind
him in the hollow formed by his back and the angle of the seat
and began to reflect on the last passage he had read:—

"The doctrine of inequality is emphatically a science of
white peoples. It is they who have invented it."

The Germans of 1854, he reflected, built up a theory of
the inferiority of the other peoples of the white race. Some
of these so-called inferior whites have, in turn, built up a
similar theory about the darker peoples. This recalled to him
some of the many falsities current about his own people. He
thought of how in nearly all the large libraries of the United
States, which he had been permitted to enter, he had found
books advancing all sorts of theories to prove that they were
inferior. He thought of the discussions he had heard on the
cars and other places from time to time, and of what he called
"the heirloom ideas" that many persons had concerning the
different varieties of the human race. These discussions, he
recalled, had done him good. They had been the means of his
acquiring a fund of knowledge on the subject of race, as they

FROM "SUPERMAN" TO MAN

had caused him to look up those opinions he had thought incorrect in the works of the standard scientists. Moved by these thoughts he took a morocco-bound notebook from his vest pocket and wrote:—"This doctrine of racial superiority apparently incited the other white peoples, most of whom were enemies to one another, to unite against the Germans in 1914. Will the doctrine of white superiority over the darker races produce a similar result to white empire?"

Suddenly the curtains parted and someone entered the room. Dixon looked up. It was a man in pajamas, slippered feet, and overcoat.

At sight of him Dixon had an unpleasant sensation. During the afternoon, this man, who, from what Dixon could gather, was a United States senator from Oklahoma, was discussing the race question with another in the smoker. Dixon had heard him say, vehemently. "The 'nigger' is a menace to our civilization and should be kept down. I am opposed to educating him, for the educated 'nigger' is a misfit in the white man's civilization. He is a caricature and no good can result from his 'butting in' on our affairs. Would to God that none of the breed had ever set foot on the shores of our country. That's the proper place for a 'nigger'," he had said quite loud, on seeing Dixon engaged in wiping out the wash bowls.

At another time he had said, "You may say what you please, but I would never eat with a 'nigger.' I couldn't stomach it. God has placed an insuperable barrier between black and white that will ever prevent them from living on the same social plane, at least so far as the Anglo-Saxon is concerned. I have no hatred for the black man—in fact, I could have none, but he must stay in his place."

"That's nothing else but racial antipathy," his opponent had objected.

"You don't have to take my word for it," said the other, snappily. "Didn't Abraham Lincoln say: 'There is a physical difference between the white and black races which, I believe, will forbid the two races living together on terms of social and political equality?' Call it what you will, but there is an indefinable something within me that tells me that I am infinitely better than the best 'nigger' that ever lived. The feeling is instinctive and I am not going to violate nature."

On hearing this, Dixon had said to himself, "My good man, how easily I could define that 'indefinable feeling' of which you speak. I notice from your positive manner, and impatience of contradiction that you experience that indefinable feeling of superiority not only towards Negroes, but toward your white associates as well and that feeling you, yourself, would call in any one else conceit.' "

Dixon had happened to be present at the close of the discussion, which had been brought to an end by the announcement of dinner. The anti-Negro passenger had had the last word. He had said:

"You, too, had slavery in the North, but it didn't pay and you gave it up. Wasn't your pedantic and self-righteous Massachusetts the first to legalize slavery? You, Northerners, forced slavery on us, and when you couldn't make any more money on it, because England had stopped the slave trade, you made war on us to make us give it up. A matter of climate, that's all. Climes reversed, it would have been the South that wanted abolition. It was a matter of business with you, not sentiment. You Northerners, who had an interest in slavery, were bitterly opposed to abolition. It is all very well for you to talk, but if you Yankees had the same percentage of 'niggers' that we have, you would sing a different tune. The bitterest people against the 'nigger' are you Northerners who have come South. You, too, have race riots, lynching and segregation. The only difference between South and North is, that one is frank and the other hypocritical," and he added with vehement sincerity, "I hate hypocrisy."

In spite of this avowed enmity toward his people, Dixon had felt no animosity toward the man. Here, he had thought, was a conscience, honest but uneducated.

Shortly afterwards another man who had been in the smoker had met Dixon in the aisle. With a laugh and a few terrible but good-natured oaths, he had said "That fellow is obsessed by the race problem. I met him yesterday at the hotel, and he has talked of hardly anything else since. This morning we were in the elevator, when a well-dressed Negro, who looked like a professional man, came in, and at once he began to tell

FROM "SUPERMAN" TO MAN

me so that all could hear him something about 'nigger' doctors in Oklahoma. If he could only see how ridiculous he is he'd shut up."

"I feel myself as good as he," he went on, "and I have associated with colored people. We have a colored porter in our office—Joe—and we think the world of him. He doesn't like 'niggers,' eh?" With a knowing wink, and nudging Dixon in the ribs, he added, "I wager his instinctive dislike, as he calls it, doesn't include both sexes of your race. I know his kind well."

Dixon had felt like saying, "We must be patient with the self-deluded," but he didn't. He had simply thanked the other for his sentiments.

All of this ran through Dixon's mind when he saw the pajama-clad passenger appear in the doorway. The latter walked up to the mirror, looked at himself quizzically a moment, then selected a chair and adjusting it to his fancy made himself comfortable in it. Then he took a plain and well-worn gold cigarette case from his pocket, selected a cigarette, and began rummaging his pockets for a match, all in apparent oblivion of Dixon at the far end of the long seat. But Dixon, who had been quietly observing him, deftly presented a lighted match, saying at the time in a respectful and solicitous tone:

"Can't sleep, sir?"

"No, George," was the reply, amiable but condescending. "I was awakened at the last stop and can't go back to sleep. I never do very well the first night out, anyway. He went on to speak about Oklahoma, and was soon talking freely. Presently he began to tell about the Negroes in his state, using words as "darkies," "niggers," and "coons."

Then he grew entertaining and began telling jokes about chicken-stealing, razor-fights, and watermelon feasts among Negroes. Of such jokes he evidently had an abundant stock, but nearly all of which Dixon had heard over and over.

One joke which he seemed especially to enjoy telling was about a Negro head-waiter in a Northern hotel. When asked by a Southern guest whether he was the "head-nigger," the head-waiter grew indignant. "Oh," said the guest, "I only wanted to know because I have a large tip for the "head-nigger." At that the head-waiter promptly got off his horse. "Yessah, boss," he said, "I'se de head-niggah, an' if yu' don' b'leeve me ast all dem othah niggahs deh,' he said, pointing to the waiters.

The senator was laughing immoderately, and Dixon laughed heartily, too. Had the senator been a mind reader, however, he would hardly have been flattered at what he considered his prowess as a jokesmith. Dixon was saying to himself, "The idea of some folks at being courteous and setting other people at their ease is so crude that it enters the realm of high comedy."

While the senator was still laughing, the train began to slow down, and Dixon, asking to be excused, slid to the other end of the seat to look out, thus leaving the book he had placed behind him, exposed. The senator saw the book, and his laughter soon changed to curiosity.

The volume stood end up on the seat and he could discern from its size and binding that it might contain serious thought. Did it? He had somehow felt that this Negro was above the ordinary and the sight of the book confirmed the feeling.

A certain forced quality in the timbre of Dixon's laughter, as also the merry twinkle in his eye, had made him feel at times just a bit uncomfortable. His curiosity getting the better of him, he reached over to take the volume, but at the same instant Dixon's slipping back to his former seat caused him to hesitate. Yet he determined to find out. He demanded flippantly, pointing to the book,—"Reading the Bible, George?"

"No, sir."

"What then?"

"Oh, only a scientific work," said the other, carelessly, not wishing to broach the subject of racial differences that the title of the book suggested.

Dixon's evident desire to evade a direct answer sharpened his curiosity. He suggested off-handedly, but with ill-concealed eagerness: "Pretty deep stuff, eh? Who's the author?"

Dixon saw the persistent curiosity in his eye. Knowing too well the type of the man before him, he did not wish to give him the book, but unable to find further pretext for withholding it, he took it from the seat, turned it right side up, and handed it over. The senator took it with feigned indifference. Moistening his forefinger, he turned over the leaves, then settled down to read the marked passages. Now and then he would mutter:

FROM "SUPERMAN" TO MAN

"Nonsense! Ridiculous!" Suddenly in a burst of impatience he turned to the frontispiece, and exclaimed in open disgust: "Just as I thought. Written by a Frenchman." Then, before he could recollect to whom he was talking—so full was he of what he regarded as the absurdity of Finot's view—he demanded—"Do you believe all this rot about the equality of the races?"

Dixon's policy was to avoid any topic that was likely to produce a difference of opinion with a passenger, provided it did not entail any sacrifice of his self-respect. He regarded his questioner as one to be humored, rather than vexed. He remembered a remark, made by this legislator that afternoon:

"The Jew, the Frenchman, the Dago and the Spaniards are all 'niggers' to a greater or less extent. The only white people are the Anglo-Saxon, Teutons and Scandinavians." This, Dixon surmised, accounted for the remark he had made about Finot's adopted nationality, and it amused him.

Dixon pondered the question. Then there occurred to him a way by which he could retain his own opinion and yet be in apparent accord with the passenger. He responded:

"No, sir, I do not believe in the equality of the races. As you say, it is impossible."

The senator looked up as if he had not been expecting a response; but, seemingly pleased with Dixon's acquiescence, he continued as he turned the leaves: "Writers of this type don't know what they are talking about. They write from mere theory. If they had to live among 'niggers,' they would sing an entirely different tune."

Dixon felt that he oughtn't to let this remark go unchallenged. He protested courteously: "Yet, sir, M. Finot had proved his argument admirably. I am sure if you were to read this book you would agree with him, too."

The senator looked up.

"Didn't you just say you didn't agree with this book?" he questioned sharply.

"I fear you misunderstood me, sir."

"Didn't you say you did not believe in the equality of the races?"

"Yes, sir."

"Then why?"

FROM "SUPERMAN" TO MAN

"Because as you said, sir, it is impossible."

"Why? Why?

"Because there is but one race—the human race."

The senator did not respond. Though angry at the manner in which Dixon had received and responded to his question, he stopped to ponder the situation in which his unwitting question had placed him. As he had confessed, he did not like educated Negroes, and had no intention of engaging in a controversy with one. His respect and his aversion for this porter increased with a bound. Now he was weighing which was the better of the two possible courses—silence and response. If he said nothing, this Negro might think he had silenced him, while to respond would be to engage in an argument, thus treating the Negro as an equal. After weighing the matter for some time he decided that silence was the less compatible with his racial dignity, and with much condescension, his stiff voice and haughty manner a marked contrast to his jollity of a few minutes past, he demanded:

"You say there is only one race. What do you call yourself?'

"An American citizen," responded the other, composedly.

"Perhaps you have never heard of the word, 'nigger'?"

"Couldn't help it, sir," said Dixon, evenly.

"Then, do you believe the 'nigger' is the equal of the Anglo-Saxon race?" he demanded with ill-concealed anger.

"I have read many books on anthropology, sir, but I have not seen mention of either a 'nigger' race or an Anglo-Saxon one."

"Very well, do you believe your race—the black race—is equal to the Caucasian?"

Dixon stopped to weigh the wisdom of his answering. What good would it do to talk with a man seemingly so rooted in his prejudices? Then a simile came to him. On a visit to the Bureau of Standards at Washington, D. C., he had seen the effect of the pressure of a single finger upon a supported bar of steel three inches thick. The light strain had caused the steel to yield one-twenty-thousandth part of an inch, as the delicate apparatus, the interferometer, had registered. Since every action, he went on to reason, produces an effect, and truth, with the impulse of the Cosmos behind it, is irresis-

tible, surely if he advanced his views in a kindly spirit, he
must modify the error in this man. But still he hesitated.
Suddenly he recalled that here was a legislator, one, who, above
all others, ought to know the truth. This decided him. He
would answer to the point, but would restrict any conversation
that might ensue to the topic of the human race as a whole.
Above all he would steer clear of the color question in the
United States. He said with soft courtesy:

"I have found, sir, that any division of humanity according
to physique, can have but a merely nominal value, as differences in physiques are caused by climatic conditions and are
subject to a rechange by them. As you know, both Science
and the Bible are agreed that all so-called races came from
a single source. Pigmented humanity becomes lighter in the
temperate zone, while unpigmented humanity becomes brown
in the tropics. One summer's exposure at a bathing beach is
enough to make a life-saver darker than many Indians. The
true skin of all human beings is of the same color: all men
are white under the first layer.

"Then it is possible by the blending of human varieties to
produce innumerable other varieties, each one capable of re-
producing and continuing itself.

"Again, anthropologists have never been able to classify
human varieties. Huxley, as you know, named 2, Blumenbach 5,
Burke 63, while others, desiring greater accuracy, have named
hundreds. Since these classifications are so vague and change-
able, it is evident, is it not, sir, that any division of humanity,
whether by color of skin, hair or facial contour, to be other
than purely nominal, must be one of mentality? And to
classify humanity by intellect, would be, as you know, an impossible task. Nature, so far as we know, made only the
individual. This idea has been ably expressed by Lamarck,
who, in speaking of the human race says,—'Classifications are
artificial, for nature has created neither classes, nor orders,
nor families, nor kinds, nor permanent species, but only individuals.'"

The senator handed back the book to Dixon, huffily. "But,
you have not answered my question," he insisted, "I asked, do

FROM "SUPERMAN" TO MAN

you believe the black race will ever attain the intellectual standard of the Caucasian?"

"Intellect, whether of civilized or uncivilized humanity, as you know, sir, is elastic in quality. That is, primitive man when transplanted to civilization not only becomes civilized, but sometimes excels some of those whose ancestors have had centuries of culture, and the child of civilized men when isolated among primitives becomes one himself. We would find that the differences between a people who had acquired say three or four generations of beneficient culture, and another who had been long civilized would be about the same as that between the individuals in the long civilized group. That is, the usual human differences would exist. To be accurate we would have to appraise each individual separately. Any comparison between the groups would be inexact."

"But," reiterated the other, sarcastically, "you have not answered my question. Do you believe the black man will ever attain the high intellectual standard of the Caucasian? Yes or no."

"For the most authoritative answer," responded Dixon in the calm manner of the disciplined thinker, "we must look to modern science. If you don't mind, sir, I will give you some quotations from scientists of acknowledged authority, all of your own race."

Dixon drew out his notebook.

"Bah," said the other savagely, "opinions! Mere opinions! I asked you what you think and you are telling me what someone else says. What I want to know is, what do YOU think."

"Each of us," replied Dixon, evenly, "however learned, however independent, is compelled to seek the opinion of someone else on some particular subject at some time. There is the doctor and the other professionals, for instance. Now in seeking advice one usually places the most reliance on those one considers experts, is it not? This afternoon I overheard you quoting from one of Lincoln's debates with Douglas in order to prove your views."

Silence.

FROM "SUPERMAN" TO MAN

Dixon opened his notebook, found the desired passage, and said:

"In 1911 most of the leading sociologists and anthropologists of the world met in a Universal Races Congress in London. The opinion of that congress was that all the so-called races of men are essentially equal. Gustav Spiller, its organizer and secretary, voiced the findings of that entire body of experts when, after a careful weighing of the question of superiority and inferiority, he said (here Dixon read from the notebook):

"'We are then under the necessity of concluding that an impartial investigator would be inclined to look upon the various important peoples of the world as, to all intents and purposes, essentially equal in intellect, enterprise, morality and physique.'"

Dixon found another passage and said: "Finot, whose findings ought to be regarded as more valuable than the expressions of those who base their arguments on sentiment or on Hebrew mythology, says,—'All peoples may attain this distant frontier which the brains of the whites have reached.' He also says:

"'The conclusion, therefore, forces itself upon us, that there are no inferior and superior races, but only races and peoples living outside or within the influence of culture.

"'The appearance of civilization and its evolution among certain white peoples and within a certain geographical latitude is only the effect of circumstances.'

"Zamenhof, the inventor of Esperanto, in his paper before the Universal Races Congress, says:

"'Give the Africans without any mingling of rancor or oppression, a high and humane civilization, and you will find their mental level will not differ from ours. Abolish the whole of our civilization and our minds will sink to the level of an African cannibal. It is not a difference of mentality in the race, but a difference of instruction.'"

Dixon closed his note-book and said, "The so-called savage varieties of mankind are the equal of the civilized varieties in this:—there is latent within them the same possibilities of development. Then the more developed peoples have the

FROM "SUPERMAN" TO MAN

germ of decay more or less actively at work within them."

The senator had been awaiting his turn with impatience. Now drawing up his overcoat over his pajama-clad knees, and raising his voice in indignation, he flung at Dixon, apparently forgetting all previous qualms of lowered racial pride, "That's all nonsense. It is not true of the Negro, for while the white, red and yellow races have, or have had, civilizations of their own, the black has had none. All he has even accomplished has been when driven by the whites. Indigenous to a continent of the greatest natural resources, he has all these ages produced absolutely nothing. Geographical position has had absolutely nothing to do with it, or we would not have had Aztec civilization. Tell me, has the Negro race ever produced a Julius Caesar, a Shakespeare, a Montezuma, a Buddha, a Confucius? The Negro and all the Negroid races are inherently inferior. It is idiocy to say the Negro is the equal of the Caucasian. God Almighty made black to serve white. He placed an everlasting curse on all the sons of Ham and the black man shall forever serve the white." His face flushed with excitement.

Dixon was apparently unmoved. He responded with courtesy, his well-modulated voice and even tones in sharp contrast to the bluster and hysteria of the other. "The belief that the history of the Negro began with his slavery in the New World, while popular, is highly erroneous. The black man, like the Aztec, was civilized when the dominant branches of the Caucasian variety were savages. You will remember sir, that Herodotus, the Father of History, an eye-witness, distinctly mentions the black skins, and woolly hair of the Egyptians of his day. In Book II, Chapter 104, of his history he says:

" 'I believe the Colchians are a colony of Egyptians, because like them they have black skin and woolly hair.'

"Aristotle in his 'Physiognomy,' Chapter VI, distinctly mentions the Ethiopians as having woolly hair and the Egyptians as being black-skinned. Count M. C. de Volney, author of 'The Ruins of Empire,' says:

" 'The ancient Egyptians were real Negroes of the same species as the other present natives of Africa.'

FROM "SUPERMAN" TO MAN

"A glance at the Sphinx or at any of the ancient Egyptian statues in the British Museum will confirm these statements. When I saw the statue of Amenemphet III, I was immediately struck by the facial resemblance to Jack Johnson. I have seen Negroes here and in Africa, who bore a striking resemblance to Seti the Great. The latter was worshipped as the god, Amen, on whose name good white Christians still call. By the light of modern research it does appear as if white-skinned humanity got its civilization from the black-skinned variety, and even its origin. Volney says:

" 'To the race of Negroes . . . the object of our extreme contempt . . we owe our arts, sciences and even the very use of speech!'

"And with reference to the production of great men by the Negro . . ."

The senator had been fidgeting in his chair. He interrupted testily, "But what about the Negro's low, debased position in the scale of civilization? Look at the millions of Negroes in Africa little better than gorillas! They are still selling their own flesh and blood, eating human flesh and carrying on their horrible voodoo! All of the white race is civilized and all the other races, to some extent. Consider the traditions of the white man and all it means! Look at the vast incomprehensible achievements of the white man,—the railroads, the busy cities, the magnificent edifices, the wireless telegraph, the radio, the ships of the air,—yes, consider all the marvels of science! What has the white man not done? He has weighed the atom and the star with perfect accuracy. He has probed the uttermost recesses of infinity and fathomed the darkest mysteries of the ocean; he has challenged the lightning for speed and equalled it; he has competed with the eagle in the air, and outstripped him; he has rivalled the fish in his native element. In fact, there is not one single opposing force in Nature that he has not bent to his adamant will. He has excelled even the excellence of Nature. Consider, too, the philosophies, the religions, the ennobling works of art and of literature. Has the Negro anything to compare? Has he anything at all to boast of? Nothing! And yet in the face of all of these overwhelming facts, things patent to even the

FROM "SUPERMAN" TO MAN

most ignorant, you tell me the Negro is the equal of the breed of supermen—wondermen—I represent? Really this childlike credulity of yours reaches the acme of absurdity. More than ever do I perceive á Negro is incapable of reasoning."

He caught for breath as he lolled back in the chair, and a smile of supreme satisfaction lit his features.

Dixon, who had been listening patiently, was seemingly unaffected. He responded composedly:—"The white man's civilization is only a continuation of that which was passed on to him by the Negro, who has simply retrogressed. 'Civilizations,' as Spiller has pointed out, 'are meteoric, bursting out of obscurity only to plunge back again.' Macedonia, for example! In our own day we have seen the decline of Aztec and Inca civilizations. Of the early history of man we know nothing definite. Prior even to paleolithic man there might have been civilizations excelling our own. In the heart of Africa, explorers may yet unearth marks of some extinct Negro civilization in a manner similar to the case of Assyria forgotten for two thousand years, and finally discovered by accident under forty feet of earth. For instance, the Chicago Evening Post of Oct. 11, 1916, speaking editorially of the discoveries made at Nepata by Dr. Reisner of Harvard, says—"To his amazement he found even greater treasures of the Ethiopian past. Fragment after fragment was unearthed until at least he had reconstructed effigies of no less than eleven monarchs of the forgotten Negro empire." Since then the tombs of fourteen other kings and fifty-five queens have been unearthed by the Reisner expedition. Among them is that of King Tirkaqua, mentioned in the book of Isaiah. An account of this appeared in the New York Times, November 27, 1921. Again, great Negro civilizations like that of Timbuctoo flourished even in the Middle Ages. Then there have been such purely Negro civilizations as that of Uganda and Songhay, which were of high rank. Boas says in his 'Mind of Primitive Man' (here Dixon took out his notebook): 'A survey of African tribes exhibits to our view cultural achievements of no mean order. All the different kinds of activities that we consider desirable in the citizens of our country may be found in aboriginal Africa.' "

FROM "SUPERMAN" TO MAN

The senator did not reply. His eyes, narrowed to slits, were peering at Dixon piercingly. The latter, returning his gaze, continued undaunted, "Spiller also says—'The status of a race at any particular moment of time offers no index to its capacities.' How true has this been of Britons, Picts and Scots, and Huns. Nineteen hundred years ago England was inhabited by savages, who stained themselves with woad, offered human sacrifices and even practiced cannibalism. Nor is culture a guarantee against decay or Greece would not have decayed. You may be sure the Roman had the same contempt for the savages of the North, who finally conquered him and almost obliterated his civilization, as have the self-styled superior peoples of today for the less developed ones. But these undeveloped peoples should not be despised. Nature, it certainly appears, does not intend to have the whole world civilized at the same time. Even as a thrifty housewife retains a balance in the bank to meet emergencies, so Nature retains these undeveloped varieties as a reserve fund to pay the toll which civilization always exacts. Finot says that many biologists regard the Caucasian as having arrived at the limit of his evolution, and that he can go no higher without danger to his overdeveloped brain. Underdeveloped peoples, like undeveloped resources, sir, are simply Nature's bank account."

The senator readjusted his slippers and went over to the water cooler for a drink. He did not like to argue in this vein. Dixon's quiet assurance and well-bred air, too, surprised him, and made him unconsciously admit to himself that here was a Negro different from his concept of that race, and not much different from himself after all. Yet his racial pride would not permit him to be outwitted by one he regarded as an inferior in spite of that 'inferior's' apparent intelligence He would try the tactics best known to him,—the same that he had more than once used successfully with Negroes. He would outface his opponent, awe him, as it were, by his racial prestige. With this determination he returned to his seat and calmly seated himself. After a few leisurely puffs of a freshly-lighted cigarette he turned to Dixon, who had not moved, and in pretty much the same tone that a bullying lawyer would use to a timid witness, shaking an extended forefinger and

FROM "SUPERMAN" TO MAN

glaring from under his knitted eyebrows, he demanded:—

"Do you mean to tell me that you really believe the Negro is the equal of the white man? That YOU think you are as good as a white man? Come on now, none of your theories."

Dixon appeared far from being intimidated. Indeed, he was secretly amused. Carefully repressing his mirth, he asked with sprightly ingenuousness:—

"In what particular, sir?"

The senator, it appears, had not foreseen an analysis of his question, for he stammered:

"Oh, you know very well what I mean. I mean—well—well—do you feel you are the equal of a white man?"

"Your question has answered itself, sir."

"In what way?"

"Well, sir, if I could tell how a white man feels, which I would have to do to make the comparison, then it would mean that I, a Negro, have the same feelings as a white man."

No response. Silence, except for the rumbling of the train. After a short pause, Dixon continued,—"Since, as your question implies, I must use the good in me as a standard by which to measure the good in a white man, I believe that any white man, who, like myself, is endeavoring to do the right thing, is as good a man as I. And more, sir," he added in a tone of gentle remonstrance, "your question has been most uncomplimentary to yourself, for, in asking me whether I consider myself as good as a white man, you are assuming that all white men, irrespective of reputation, are alike."

The senator appeared more confused than ever. His face flushed and his eyes moved shiftily. But he was determined not to be beaten. Rallying to the charge, he began in an irritable and domineering tone: "You said you were born in Alabama?"

"Yes, sir."

"Your father was a slave, wasn't he?"

"My grandmother, sir," corrected Dixon frankly.

"Well, what I want to get at is this:—do you, the descendant of a slave, consider yourself the social equal of a white man, who has always been free, and who owned your people as chattels?" And he finished austerely: "Come on now, no more beating around the bush."

Dixon decided to accept his meaning. In a tone that implied a perfect mutual understanding, he began:—"Of course, sir, this is a matter that deeply concerns our country and humanity, and so I feel that we two can speak on it calmly and without any ill feeling." Then in a polite and convincing tone, he explained,—"Reared, as I was, in a part of the South where a white skin is deified and a black one vilified, candidly, in my childhood, I did believe that there was something about the white man that made him superior to me. But, fortunately for me, I have travelled and read considerably. I once worked for one Mr. Simpson, a lecturer. While with him I visited the principal countries of the world. In one English town, where I lived six months, I didn't see a dark face. Living thus exclusively among whites, I observed that, except for differences due entirely to environment, my people were essentially the same as the whites. Indeed, what struck me most in my travels was the universality of human nature. European-reared Negroes possessed, so far as I could discern, the same temperament and manner, class for class, as the whites, Then my position on these cars has given me a rare opportunity for continued observations. I have met white persons in all kinds of relationships, and if there is any inherent difference between Negro and Caucasian, I have failed to find it after more than thirty years of rather careful observation. It is needless to say, sir, that my ideas of superiority based on lack of pigment or texture of hair evaporated long ago."

This reply nettled the senator still more. He demanded with increased irritation, "But what about slavery? The Negro has been a slave since the dawn of history. Consult any dictionary of synonyms, and you will see the term 'Negro' is synonymous with 'slave.' A black skin has ever been a livery of servitude. Isn't this world-old slavery a sign of the Negro's hopeless inferiority? My father had hundreds of slaves!"

Dixon noticed the senator's increased agitation and determined to be calmer than ever. He replied with a blandness that exasperated the other still more:—"Strange as it may sound, sir, the Caucasian has never been really free. The vast

FROM "SUPERMAN" TO MAN

majority of its members are today, industrially, the serfs, and mentally, the slaves of the few. But, if we accept the term literally, all or nearly all branches of the white variety of mankind have been slaves that could be bought or sold. Britons were slaves to the Romans. Cicero, writing to his friend, Atticus, said,—'The stupidest and ugliest slaves come from Britain.' Later they were slaves of the Normans. Palgrave, an English historian, says of the Anglo-Saxon period:

" 'The Theowe (Anglo-Saxon slave) was entirely the property of his master, body as well as labor; like the Negro, he was part of the live stock, ranking in use and value with the beasts of the plough.'

"Villenage persisted in England until the sixteenth century. Certain classes of Anglo-Saxon slaves were not even permitted to buy their freedom, since it was contended that their all was the property of their masters. Serfdom was not abolished in Prussia until 1807, and in Austria until 1848. Even here in America white persons were slaves. There were Irish slaves in New England."

"Irish slaves in New England?" echoed the other in scornful surprise.

"Yes, sir, Irish men and women were slaves in New England, being sold like black slaves and treated not a whit better. Many of the most socially prominent in America have slave ancestors. Lincoln's ancestors were white slaves. According to Professor Cigrand, Grover Cleveland's great-grandfather, R chard Falley, was an Irish slave in Connecticut. There were also white slaves in Virginia. Black and white slaves used to work together in the fields in Barbadoes. Indeed, it would be quite possible to find white persons living in this country who were born in actual slavery, such having come from Russia, where slavery was abolished the same year our Emancipation Proclamation was signed ... Ah, and that reminds me. The word, slave, has a white origin."

"A white origin!"

"Yes, sir, it comes from 'Slav,' a very white-skinned people who were reduced to slavery by the Germans. . . ."

"Never heard of that."

"Nevertheless, sir, you'll find it in the Century, or any other standard, dictionary."

FROM "SUPERMAN" TO MAN

The senator was silent.

Dixon added: "As for Africa, white people were held slaves there for many centuries by the blacks. Read, for instance, the works of Abbe Busnot, who visited Morocco in the seventeenth century. Why, as you know, as late as 1815, white Americans were captured on the high seas and taken as slaves by the blacks into the Sudan. You probably remember, how President Madison sent Commodore Decatur and others to free them. You'll find several books in the Congressional Library written by these white American slaves, who had been freed."

The senator was silent. He had never head of these things. They seemed incredible, yet he was in no position to contradict them. He would have his secretary hunt them up as soon as he got back to Washington.

Dixon went on, "Of course, I could say much about how Negroes bought white people as slaves in this country as late as 1818. But for the honor of the Negro, I think the less said of that the better. The slave-holder, white or black, was an odious creature, at least he is in twentieth century eyes. He was either a kidnapper or an abettor of kidnapping." Remembering how the senator had been boasting of how his people had owned slaves, Dixon added, "If my people had owned slaves, I certainly wouldn't broadcast it, because slaveholders were parasites of the most pernicious kind. In so far as any stigma is attached to slavery today, it should be placed, not on the descendants of the slaves, but on those of the slaveholders."

The senator glared angrily. He was being hit in his most vital spot. The proud boast of himself and his aristocratic friends was that their fathers had held slaves. Moreover, he was exasperated at the argument but he felt himself held in it as a vise. He arose hastily, stopped, paced the smoker, then sat down again. After a few moments he insisted:

"But the Negro, himself, acknowledges his racial inferiority. Just look how he bleaches his skin, straightens his hair, and uses other devices to appear like the white man! Isn't that a sign of inferiority? Imitation is acknowledgment of superiority. Do you see any other race thus imitating the looks of the white man? I can't imagine a more comical sight than a Negro dandy with his hair all ironed out until it looks like

FROM "SUPERMAN" TO MAN

the quills upon the fretful porcupine. Imagine a white man darkening himself to look like a Negro!" Then he added, sneeringly, "The Negro is ashamed of himself. If he believes himself the equal of the white man, his actions certainly do not show it."

Dixon started. He had never looked at this matter in this light before. Now he pondered his reply.

The passenger noted his silence with a smile of satisfaction. Dixon found his response.

"Yes, these Negroes, who 'doctor' themselves to appear white do acknowledge inferiority. I have always held that one's hair or color of skin is as perfect as nature can make them, so perfect that to tamper with either is the surest way of upriling them eventually."

So much the worse for the black man, then," retorted the senator, sarcastically, "that he should try to ape a race below him. He is just inferior, that's all. The best proof is that he acknowledges it himself. When a man acknowledges his faults, don't you believe him?"

"Indeed, sir," retorted Dixon. "It is clearly the fault of the average white that these so-called Negroes should try to be other than they are. In a country where a drop of 'Negro' blood, more or less visible, and a 'kink,' more or less pronounced, in the hair may altogether change the current of one's life, what can you expect?"

Dixon paused an instant, then continued: "I will give you an instance: two brothers intimately known to me arrived in New York from abroad. The hair of one brother did not indicate Negro extraction, that of the other did. The straight-haired one obtained a position commensurate with his ability. Incidentally, he went South and married a white woman. The other, the better educated and more gentlemanly of the two, too manly for subterfuge, after fruitless endeavor, had to take a porter's job. He finally went back home in disgust."

Dixon added reflectively, "Also do not forget that if certain Negroes iron their curly hair to make it straight, certain whites also iron their straight hair to make it curly. Madame Walker, it is said, made a million dollars by straightening the hair of

FROM "SUPERMAN" TO MAN

Negroes; Monsieur Marcel made about twenty times that by the reverse process among the whites. The whites, also, by bleaching their complexion and hair, wearing false hair, and the like, not to mention the use of sun-tan lotions, make a false show too, don't they? Whose superiority are they aping then?"

The senator shifted in his seat uncomfortably! ! After a few moments he responded a shade less confidently, but with greater bluster, "What about this, then:—the Negro shows no originality, not even so far as contemptuous·epithets are concerned. The white man calls the Negro 'nigger' and yet the Negro accepts it even to the length of calling himself so. Fancy a white man calling himself by a name given to him by Negroes! The Negro is a mimic. He has the same amount of reasoning power as a poll-parrot."

"Yes," admitted Dixon, "a great number of uneducated Negroes, also a goodly number of those with mere book-learning, do act in a manner to warrant your statement. The habit that far too many Negroes have of calling themselves by those objectionable epithets given them by their white contemners cannot be too strongly condemned, and yet, isn't the surest way of nullifying a nickname to call yourself by it? Anyway, I have been to South America and the Negroes there would never think of addressing one another thus. Indeed, even a full-blooded Brazilian Negro feels hurt if called a Negro in pretty much the same way that a descendant of the Pilgrim Fathers would be if called an Englishman. The Brazilian wishes to be known solely by his national patronymic."

"Because he is ashamed of his race," retorted the passenger.

"Not necessarily," replied Dixon. "In Europe, the inhabitants do not think of themselves as white men, but as Germans, Frenchmen, etc. And in Brazil, where slavery existed as late as 1888, the Negro is taught not only to regard himself the equal of the white man, but he is given an opportunity to prove it. There is no walk of Brazilian life, official or unofficial, where he is not welcome and which he has not filled At least two Brazilian presidents were of Negro descent. In the United States, on the other hand, it does appear as if everything possible is done to humble the Negro, to suppress his self-respect. There ought to be small wonder then, if many Negroes do not show sufficient

FROM "SUPERMAN" TO MAN

manly dignity, and many others, without weighing the purport, try to appear white, an act, that, after all, somewhat parallels that of the white man who blisters himself in the sun in an endeavor to appear, no doubt, like the bronzed heroes of the story books."

The passenger did not respond. He appeared to be busily engaged in studying the inlaid woodwork. Dixon then added with assumed gravity:—

"I concede, however, sir, that the average Negro acknowledges his inferiority tacitly and often by speech."

The senator straightened up instantly. He smiled triumphantly and replied with an air of finality, "Well, that settles the argument. I knew you would finally come to the truth." He rose as if to go.

"But, in this instance," Dixon queried archly, "might not an acknowledgment of inferiority prove a certain superiority?"

"Inferiority proving superiority!" shouted the other, dropping back into his seat. "What are you saying, anyway?"

"Doesn't the case of the sexes explain this seeming paradox? The average male human, as you will admit, is egotistic. The more that woman, the weaker, humors this trait, the better she serves here own interest; similarly, the average white man's weak point is his color egotism, and the more the Negro humors this failing, the more he serves his own interest. The greater the self-interest of the woman, the more credulous she appears to tales of masculine prowess; the greater the self-interest of the Negro, the more he flatters the white man's egotism. Now, sir, who is the cleverer, the fooled or the one who fools?"

The senator did not reply.

Dixon continued, "Permit me to illustrate. One day I was in a bar in Chicago when a white man, whom I instantly recognized as a Southerner by his dress and manner, entered. Lounging in a corner was a Negro, one of those human beings who elect to live by his wits. No sooner had the Southerner ordered his drink than the Negro sidled up to him, and looking him over admiringly said, with one eye on the white man's glass, 'What a pretty white man! Say, boss, yo' is fum Mizzourah, ain't yo'?'

" 'Yes,' said the white man pleased at the open admiration, 'an' wheh ah yo' fum?'

FROM "SUPERMAN" TO MAN

" 'Ah, boss,' chided the Negro, 'how kin yo' ast me dat. Boss, Ah'll have a gin-an-rass, too. Dat'll tell yo'!' (Raspberry wine and gin, a favorite drink among certain classes in Missouri.)

"The Negro had his drink, and the white man in paying pulled out a roll of bills. The sight of so much money fired the Negro's eloquence. He redoubled his flattery, telling his host how the Northern 'niggers' were 'biggity,' how they thought themselves 'as good a white folks,' and when he had his victim flattered to the seventh heaven of delight, he sprang a hard luck story. The result was several more 'gin-an-rasses' and a dollar!"

Dixon told the story in a breezy manner, but the senator failed to see any humor in it.

"From what you say," he objected coldly, "the white man must have been very ignorant. And then might not a 'nig——' Negro permit himself to be thus flattered by a white man?"

"Possibly. But this story, and similar ones I could tell you, prove that acknowledgment of inferiority often means self-interest. The case of Booker T. Washington, however, proves a better example. Washington got along well in the South because he knew just how to tickle the color-vanity of the whites. Had he shown the assertive spirit of William Monroe Trotter, he would not have got along in the South at all. But, I am opposed to this policy of trying to gain by subterfuge or blandishment, that which is one's divine right!"

Silence for a few moments, then the senator said, "Well, how do you explain this? Negroes think themselves superior to other Negroes in proportion to the amount of Caucasian blood in their veins. If that is not an instinctive acknowledgment of inferiority I don't know what it is."

"It is true," conceded Dixon, "that many lighter-skinned Negroes do look down on their darker brothers. Many others shun them too, from economic necessity; that is, they can earn more by passing for white. But, in the first instance, can't we find a similar thing among whites? Mark you, I am not defending this inexcusable ignorance among so-called Negroes. I have always held that the man who protests against a thing should be the last man to practice it. In the United States a premium is set upon Caucasian blood (of course, I use the term figuratively), hence, some mixed bloods believe themselves of superior caste.

FROM SUPERMAN" TO MAN

In the United States, due to the absence of a nobility, a premium is set upon Mayflower descent, and many persons so descended pride themselves upon their superiority due to ancestry-—blue-bloods—F. F. V.'s, yes, even from the dark-skinned Pocahontas. Some rich American women go even further. They marry Europeans with titles, some of whom were only pimps who received social recognition.

"Again, it must be remembered that there is considerable rivalry between the brunettes and the blondes. I have heard rather heated arguments between white women of these types as to their respective merits. Blondes, having the lesser amount of pigment, are supposed to be the more virtuous, which, perhaps accounts for the large number of chemical blondes among women of your race . . . and mine, too.

"But those among us who have an infusion of Caucasian blood have nothing to boast of since such are in the position of children who have been abandoned by one of their parents. Then, too, whenever they are discovered among the whites they are always unceremoniously thrust out. In my opinion the Negro who takes pride in his white descent simply does not think."

The bell had begun to ring just as Dixon was finishing, and he went in to answer the call. He was very glad of the interruption and remained away, hoping to break off the argument, but the senator had no such intention. He simply could not quit now. When Dixon ten minutes later had occasion to re-enter the room he immediately assailed him with:

"There is another important point of Negro inferiority. The features of the Caucasian are more pleasing, not only to the Caucasian, but to the Negroes, judging from their own comments. No one would ever think of comparing the physiognomy of a Negro with that of an an Adonis or an Aphrodite. The white man's native sense of beauty will never permit him to modify his ideals." He paused, then added with conviction: "The Negro's physiognomy will ever make him unpleasing to the white man."

Dixon thought of telling him that this matter of physiognomy was the cause of all the trouble, but replied, instead: "The features of the Caucasian are, as a rule, more pleasing only to his own eye for each human variety, except when imbued with

FROM "SUPERMAN" TO MAN

the thought of another people, as say, the Negro in the New World, considers its facial casts the standard. Darwin, in his 'Descent of Man,' says that when the Negro boys on the east coast of Africa saw Burton, the explorer, they cried out:

"'Look at the *white* man! Does he not look like a white ape?'

"Winwood Reade said that the Negroes on the Western Coast admired a very black skin more than one of a lighter tint. Agbebi, a West African scientist, says in his paper before the Races Congress (here Dixon consulted his notebook):

"'The unsophisticated African entertains an aversion to white people, and when accidentally or unexpectedly meeting a white man, he turns or takes to his heels, it is because he feels that he has come upon some unusual or unearthly creature, some hobgoblin or ghost or sprite, and that an aquiline nose, scant lips, and cat-like eyes afflict him.'

"Dan Crawford, the famous African missionary, tells of an instance where a number of Negro women in Central Africa, on seeing a white man for the first time, nearly broke down a doorway in their frantic haste to escape. The Yoruba word for white man is not complimentary. It means 'peeled man.' Stanley, the explorer, said that when he returned from the wilds of Africa he found the complexions of Europeans ghastly 'after so long gazing on rich black and richer bronze.'"

The brakeman, passing by, peered into the room, but only greeted Dixon and went on.

When he was gone Dixon continued: "Oriental ideas of beauty are also different from ours. The Japanese do not like the noses and eyes of the Caucasian, which happen to be the very parts of Japanese physiognomy the Caucasians like least. Now, as Von Luschan asks, 'Which of these races is right, since both are highly artistic?'"

"But," protested the senator, rather lamely, "since the white race is the super—most developed one, its standard of beauty ought to be accepted as the universal one."

Dixon noted with satisfaction the other's hesitation at the word "superior." He laughed, "Ought, sir? Might as well say that all the rest of humanity ought to like the same kind of food and the same kind of music as the particular group that happens to be on top. But, sir, I am sure you wouldn't like that. What would happen, for instance, if the Negro male in the United States accepted only the standard you said the darker races should accept. No, you wouldn't like it. . . . Of course, I know, that peoples subjected to the beneficial influences of Science and Art have, according to the standard of civilized man, more refined features and are considered more beautiful than so-called savages.

"But facial beauty is only one side of the story. Venus and Apollo, as you will remember, are as famous for their beauty of bodily outline as for their facial contour, perhaps more so. And in a matter of bodily beauty certain African peoples easily excel the white man. The Zulus, a black people, are the successors of the ancient Greeks in beauty of physique. J. H. Balmer, explorer and lecturer, says:

" 'The Zulus are the physical superior of other races. A male Zulu has the strength, endurance and body of a prizefighter in the pink of condition. Their shoulders are broad, their chests deep, their waists slim. Their women are the strongest females propagated.'

"Incidentally, coming nearer home did you know that Dr. Sargent, physical director of Harvard University, selected an American Negro, Thomas Watson, as possessing the finest physique he had ever seen? He pronounced Watson as being superior to the Apollo Belvedere, the model of perfection in Greek statuary? Others have thought that the Greeks used Negroes as models for the body of their statues."

He did not reply. Dixon went on, "But here in America it is not a matter of facial contour or physique. It is a question of color and texture of hair, sometimes color alone, sometimes hair alone, since there are many Negroes who possess the regular profile of the conventional Caucasian whilst there are many Caucasians who, but for color and hair might be representatives of any other human variety, except the true Mongolian. I have remarked many Swedish and Irish persons with Negroid features. Then, too, the beauty of colored women commands consideration. In all those parts of the British Empire where black and white live, those women who have what is known as a 'touch of the tar-brush' easily excel the average white woman in beauty and grace of expression. The white women of these countries

FROM "SUPERMAN" TO MAN

are mostly English, and the Englishwoman, generally speaking, is not considered beautiful. And even here in America, where the blending of the various peoples and the superior economic conditions have combined to produce types perhaps of world-excelling beauty, certain types of colored women are the peers of any. The bewitching languor of form and voice, the placid depth of the soft, sparkling eye, and flawless texture of skin, combine with a disposition of artless amiability to make a charm that must move the hearts of all who venture to behold her. I must not forget to add that a large number of white people do think Negroes more beautiful than members of their own group. But I consider this question of facial beauty a wearisome one. The ultimate question has always been that of the mental and moral worth of the individual. Measured by the Greek standard of facial contour, Socrates, Herbert Spencer, Darwin, Voltaire and Steinmetz were ugly, and yet, the services they rendered to humanity are almost inestimable. Whilst ideas of beauty are purely individual, the standard of soul is universal. Character, then, should be the standard by which to judge human beings. After all, man is not like cattle which we rear for appearance' sake. I think that any face lit up by right living and high ideals is beautiful regardless of contour."

The senator seemed agitated. He got up and again paced the room. After a few turns he sat down and drew deep inhalations from his cigarette, blowing out the smoke very slowly. He was marshalling in his mind all the many points regarding Negro inferiority.

Suddenly, as if struck by an inspiration, he said triumphantly: "I can positively prove the Negro is inherently inferior. The Jews were slaves to the Egyptians who, according to you, were Negroes, for four hundred and thirty years, one hundred and eighty years longer than were the Negroes in America. Did they emerge in the debased condition of the Negro? No! Why? You also said that the Irish were slaves in New England, didn't you? Well; today these former slaves dominate the United States politically. Here's where the inferiority comes in. There are twelve millions of Negroes in the United States— a greater number than the population of Canada, greater than the combined population of Holland and Switzerland—and yet there is

FROM "SUPERMAN" TO MAN

not a single Negro in any position of political importance in this country. A few, it is true, hold federal positions, mostly unimportant, however. If the Negro were not the inferior, would he allow himself to be thus outclassed?"

"I will first answer your question about the Jews. When they emerged from slavery they had, according to the Bible, their Jehovah to perform wondrous miracles for them, feeding them free, capturing cities, etc., hadn't they? The Negro started with nothing and has had to fight his own battle every inch of the way.

"Again the Negro's inferior position isn't due to inferiority of human variety, but to inferiority in numbers."

"To inter-racial jealousy, you mean; the surest sign of a consciousness of inferiority among any people. Race prejudice only hurts those who have a consciousness of their racial inferiority. The Negro can't trust himself. He hates to associate with his own people."

"With regard to this matter of unity among my people," responded Dixon, "the first point to be considered is:—shall we have Negroes or shall we have Americans? We can't have both. The closer certain nationalities in our population get together the further they drift from what ought to be the predominating idea—the general welfare of the State. I think that the aim of the Negro should be national, not segregated, unity; provided, of course, that the white man will permit him. Why should a certain class of citizens band themselves in a separate camp, patronizing only themselves, working only among themselves, and so on? Let us suppose that the Jews, the Irish, the May-flower descendants, and others, form themselves into their respective camps, patronizing only themselves. Wouldn't it make for narrowness, not to say national disharmony? None of the nationalities that come here are forced to segregate themselves—indeed, they are upbraided when they do so, as listen to the fuss that is made about the German-American. Another point:—too close a Negro unity makes for segregation. And with regard to Negroes not acting more in unity, the truth is you can never get any group of human beings to think alike, not even to act alike, even when their most vital interests are concerned. Hitler has been eating up the European nations one after the other, yet haven't they played a lone hand instead of standing together? "Again, in California a great racket is made about the Japanese, yet isn't it the whites who are their main support? The Gentile has complained for centuries about the Jew, yet doesn't he go on dealing with him just the same? And there are even those Negroes who defend the Caucasian in his treatment of their people. Among my people I notice that those who preach what they call racial unity do not practice it when it affects their pocketbooks. Just as long as the Negro has the same ideals and ideas as the whites, is as easily pacified, and remains as credulous as he is, I do not think that he will be more united than at present. On the other hand, I think there are three reasons why the Negro should spend his money among his own people; first, a matter of personal pride, for the majority of the white persons whom he patronizes really despise him in their hearts; second, his is a struggling group and needs support; and third, since he is forced to work for the whites for smaller than the usual wage, he should not spend it with them at the normal rate. Moreover, you must not forget that the principal supporters of Negro business are Negroes."

The senator drew his overcoat closer around him. Dixon noticed his motion and asked if he were cold.

"Somewhat," was the reply. Dixon reached under the seat and turned on the steam. A few minutes later when the steam was thumping in the pipes, the senator said: "The Negro is a whiner. He is always whining, whining. He would do better by not protesting so much."

"Sir," replied Dixon, "it's very evident that since the Negro's disparity in numbers and wealth makes it impossible to take up arms for his rights, at least at this time, he must follow the course pursued by all peoples at a similar disadvantage, that is, protest."

"But the race loses valuable time in protesting—time that could be employed in bettering its condition."

"Losing time by protesting! Can't you imagine King George and his supporters making just such an argument against the American colonists when they protested against unjust taxes? If the Negro were to say nothing wouldn't it most naturally be taken that he is contented? I do consider it the duty not only

FROM "SUPERMAN" TO MAN

of those who suffer from, but also those who see injustice, to protest against it. Did not Christ denounce the Pharisees and the rich with all the might of his soul? When the Jews were rebuilding the walls of Jerusalem on their return from Babylonian captivity did they not build sword in one hand and trowel in the other? Consider this also: at school the spirit of the Declaration of Independence is instilled into us. We are taught to admire bold, indomitable spirits like Julius Caesar, William Tell, Patrick Henry, and George Washington. We are expected to be brave in war, in short, all the standards of the whites are impressed upon us. Do you suppose then we can remain passive whilst our most elementary rights are trampled upon? Has taxation without representation ceased to be tyranny?

"Again look at the large number of discontented native whites who are bitterly fighting, and who already have what Negroes are fighting for! There are the La Follettes, the Hiram Johnsons, the Nyes, Browders, and Scott Nearings. Why not the DuBoises, the Trotters, the Fords and the Randolphs? But this objection to our protesting is a hopeful sign; it shows that conscience is at work."

Dixon reflected an instant and continued: "A similar number of whites would undoubtedly take more active measures to gain their rights, but the Negro, not much educated and without efficient organization, is almost helpless and has to plead for that which he might demand were he united. He represents not less than one-ninth of the population, yet, as you say, there is not a single one in the higher councils of the nation. The truth is that the Negro, like the Irish in Ireland, lacks that spirit of give and take usually found among oppressed peoples like the Bohemians and the Jews. Inter-racial jealousy, as you said. Like the Irish, we are a race of individualists."

"Then all the other nationalities get ahead of the Negro," said the senator. "Look at the Italians, the Polacks and all the others!"

"Your analogy isn't fair."

"Can't see why."

"These people are all white," replied Dixon, "and however hard the first generation may find it—such extra hardships being due almost entirely to their own deficiencies—the second

one or so blends with the rest of the whites. The Negro, however, is regarded as a separate entity. Another point, sir, the
immigrant not only gets ahead of the Negro, but of the native
whites as well. Just look at names on the signs along any
business street or in any directory! Indeed, the most American
group of whites is the most decadent of all,—for example the
whites of the Southern States, like Georgia and Tennessee. The
most progressive Northern States are those that have received
the greatest proportion of immigration, like New York, Penn-
sylvania and Massachusetts; the least progressive those that have
received little, like Maine and New Hampshire. The same holds
true of the Western ones. The least progressive of all the
groups that make up our cosmopolitan population happens to be
the Anglo-Saxon. I refer directly to the poor white mountaineers
of Kentucky and Tennessee. Albert Bushnell Hart in his book,
'The Southern South,' compares them with the peoples of New
England in the seventeenth century. Then, there are the poor
native whites of good Anglo-Saxon stock living in places like
Clinton and Franklin Counties, New York; Aristook County,
Maine; and Windham County, Connecticut. Professor Branson,
of North Carolina, compares these people to those crab-like
creatures mentioned in 'Les Miserables'; people, who, before
advancing light, steadily retreat into the fringe of darkness'—
while the Chicago Journal, Oct. 3, 1916, wonders if they are not
beyond the help of education. These poor and decadent whites,
North as well as South, are, as I said, the purest representatives
of that Anglo-Saxon race that the Watsons, Vardamans and Rod-
denberrys are always bragging about. They are a striking example of decay. Most communities of them are no better than
primitive African ones, and certainly much below a people like
the Basutos. You spoke of inferior races; here, if anywhere on
earth, is one.

"The Negro, however, is growing out of the ideas inculcated
in slavery. Each succeeding generation will be progressively
assertive of its manhood. I repeat, all that the group lacks is
training and opportunity."

"No amount of training will ever make him anything else
but a Negro," snapped the senator, "he is simply incapable of

FROM "SUPERMAN" TO MAN

governing himself. Who evolved the white man's government for him? Look what a miserable failure Liberia has been amid the wealth of the vast African continent! Look what a farce Haiti is! There never has been a successful government by Negroes and there never will be one. I'd give you a hundred dollars just to name a single one."

"As you justly observed, sir, the white man's government has been a matter of evolution. The nucleus was passed on to him by darker peoples, most of whom have passed away with time. Consider the painful evolution of the British Government, undoubtedly the most stable and best functioning one today. Well, the Britons, after four hundred and sixty-four years of Roman rule lapsed into barbarism when Rome left them to govern themselves. Lang says that the Picts and Dalridiac Scots, after driving out the English, fell into a quadrangular warfare among themselves. Doesn't this sound like Mexico and Haiti in the unsettled 1910's? And as regards Liberia, think what would have happened to Virginia and New England, if they had received as little support from the mother-land as Liberia has had."

"But Mexico and Haiti had the examples of the well governed countries to go by."

"Well, in the same sense, so had the English," said Dixon, "but it was not until the reign of Edward III that England began to have a settled government, and it took infusion after infusion of superior civilizations—Saxons, Danes, Normans, Gascons— to make that government. It was not until the beginning of Victoria's reign that the British government was firmly established—fully two thousand years after the landing of Julius Caesar.

"Government, like everything else on earth, is a process of evolution. As mankind through all the ages appears ever the same the state of less developed peoples affords the more highly developed ones a fine opportunity to observe the stages through which they have come, in the same manner that the old man by watching the growing child can see himself again. England, as you will recall, had civil war after civil war, one of which, the War of the Roses, lasted for thirty years. The Negro played his part before the white man came on the stage, and will very likely play it again when he is gone. Apart from old Egypt

FROM "SUPERMAN" TO MAN

there have been several successful Negro governments like Timbuctoo, Songhay, and Uganda. The last thrived for more than five centuries and well into our day until annexed by the British. When Speke discovered Uganda he said that the people had developed a high state of civilization, and 'Chinese' Gordon speaks cordially of the fine government of King Mtesa. Stanley in 'The Dark Continent' speaking of King Mtesa's court says: 'The most courtly European could not have excelled the Uganda premier.' "

The senator made no immediate reply. He was anxious to find some bad trait peculiar to black men. His mind ran over the conventional list. First he thought of rape, but he had read the Bible and knew the first rapes in that record had been committed by white men. He had also sat on juries where white men had been sentenced for this crime. He also remembered the treatment that Negro women had received at the hands of white man during slavery and it made him fear to bring up this question. His opponent, he felt, had been too skillful in finding parallels between white and black.

He next thought of the question of mendacity: white men were not always truthful either. He thought of stealing; but he had had several business adventures and he had to acknowledge that white men were princes of theft compared with Negroes. He turned to sexual immorality; here he hesitated as thoughts of the mulatto came into his mind. Visions of the big city's tenderloin districts flashed before him, as well as the statistics of illegitimacy among whites. But having heard so often that Negroes were more immoral than whites he decided to speak of Negro immorality. Striking out boldly, he said: "The highest sign of the culture of a race is the control that race exercises over the animal passions by the sheer power of its intelligence; isn't it?"

"Yes," replied Dixon, "True culture is built upon a certain measure of restraint, that is, a cultured man remembers that others have feelings like himself. Because of this, he restrains his egotism, individual or racial, religious or national."

"I said, 'animal passions!' "

"Isn't egotism an animal passion? What is more egotistic than a hog or a cat, except certain human beings?"

FROM "SUPERMAN" TO MAN

"Very well, then, I mean sexual passions. The white race is immeasurably superior in that respect. The Negro has no more ideas of morality than a monkey; in fact, he is non-moral." And he went on at some length to tell of his experiences.

"Oh, you were thinking of sexual morality and I of ethical. But here also it is impossible to make any assertion as to the sexual morals of any people with any degree of accuracy. Negroes hold, too, quite as bad an opinion of Caucasian morality. I have seen on sleeping cars and in hotels incidents among the whites similar to what you have just told me. Our nearest guide in this matter must be the opinions of unprejudiced scientists. And before I go any further I want to remind you that you said Negroes were non-moral as I shall come to that later.

"Havelock Ellis, famous authority on sex, in 'Studies in the Psychology of Sex' (Vol. 3), after giving two convincing reasons in favor of the so-called savage, says:

" 'It is a common notion that the Negro and the Negroid races of Africa are prone to sexual indulgence. This notion is not supported by those who have the most intimate knowledge of these people. It probably gained currency in part from the open and expansive temperament of the Negro and in part from the extreme sexual character of many African orgies and festivals.'

"I might add one of my own reasons to Ellis';—the belief of so-called civilized folk that lack of clothes makes for immorality.

"Finot says, 'These accusations must fall before facts.'

"Mary Gaunt, in 'Alone in West Africa' says,—

" 'There is not in all the length and breadth of Africa, I venture to swear, one-quarter of the unutterable misery and vice you may see any day in the streets of London or any great city of the British Isles. There is not a tribe that has not its own system of morality and sees that it is carried out.' "

The senator did not reply so Dixon continued: "I have another quotation from Havelock Ellis as follows:—

" 'The importance even sacredness of procreation is much more generally recognized by savages than by civilized peoples, and also a certain symbolic significance is attached to human procreation as related to natural fruitfulness generally, so that a primitive orgy, instead of being a mere manifestation of licentiousness may have a ritual significance.' "

FROM "SUPERMAN" TO MAN

"But that does not mean the Negro in the United States," objected the senator. "No one can ever tell me that the Negro is not far more lustful than the Anglo-Saxon. The Negro's lustfulness will ever prevent his being of any consequence. Negro boys and girls learn well up to a certain age, but their strong lascivious nature—that trait that links them closely with the ape—will ever make them the inferior of white children."

"What you say of the morality of the Negro is partly true, sir, but let me ask you: What do you think would happen if all the colored women in the United States suddenly decided to become very chaste? Would the Southern white man relish that? You know as well as I do that the white man has had the chief hand in undermining the morals of Negro women. He has been living in concubinage with them for over three hundred years! Wouldn't that spoil the morals of any people, however pure originally?"

"Nothing will ever persuade me that the Caucasian can in any way approach the lustfulness of the black." And he went on to give illustrations.

"I'm inclined the believe that the sex instinct is more highly developed among the whites, at least, certain classes of them. These I have in mind are individualistic and have greater difficulty in finding their sexual mates. A great deal, if not the greater part, of the deep discontent and restlessness of cultured white women is due to this. Hence they are conscious, very conscious of sex. In addition, Havelock Ellis seems to prove that the more developed a people, the stronger the sex instinct. The Negro, again, eats less stimulating food, works more laboriously, and has less leisure than the white man. The whites, on the other hand, have more uplifting diversions. I spoke then of the middle class white, for I believe that the very lowest type of Negro, is, in this respect, superior to a certain class among the whites. I mean the idle rich. The Negroes are so, not because of any inherent virtue but simply because they must use up a great deal of this energy in toil while the idle rich doesn't. It is a matter of the most common knowledge that the idle aristocrats of all climes and all ages are the most lascivious and perverted group in any country."

"You will admit at least that race for race the white man

FROM "SUPERMAN" TO MAN

has higher ideals of sexual morality than the black," said the senator.

"Yes, but you are forcing me to say what I have been trying to avoid saying ever since you gave me the cue of 'non-morality.'"

"Well?"

"You said Negroes were non-moral. On the other hand you said that the whites had higher ideas of morality. Now, if the man with high ideals *acts* in the same manner as the man that never was taught any morals—well? Is it necessary for me to say any more? The plain truth is that civilized man with his higher intellectual development uses that development to invent forms of vice far beyond the consciousness of primitive man."

Dixon consulted his notebook a moment and said: "I have a quotation here from the Medical Review of Reviews for July 1916. The editor in speaking of the report of the Baltimore Vice Commission, says:—

"'It tells a tale of lust and sexual deceit and whoredom among the most reputable Baltmoreans—it lifts the cover from a never-ceasing cauldron of sensuality and seduction. Baltimore is a city taken in adultery. . . . The twelve hundred pages of this report are a transcript of the white man's sexual life anywhere: a record that ought to prevent him from criticizing other races.'

"Chicago had a similar investigation in 1910. The report on vice, as published from the account books of white houses of prostitution, is enough to make Satan himself shiver. The number of men each woman had on single nights was given. One sixteen year-old girl served 130 men in five nights, while one veteran had sixty in a single night at fifty cents each. You will find that in the "Social Evil in Chicago," published by the Vice Commission of Chicago, pages 97-98, 3rd edition, 1911.

"But Negro women are very immoral," persisted the senator. He illustrated his viewpoint with lurid examples.

"I have no reason to doubt your experiences, sir, but similar tales can be told of Caucasian women. Isn't it they who pose for those lewd pictures of which the late Anthony Comstock had so remarkable a collection?"

The senator did not reply so Dixon continued: "A French Army Surgeon, who spent thirty years in the tropics and made

FROM "SUPERMAN" TO MAN

a study of Negro primitive women, says in his "Untrodden Fields of Anthropology': 'I must in the first place do my best to destroy the common impression that the Negro woman is very passionate. She is nothing of the kind.' He goes on to speak of 'the contempt of the Negro woman for the white man' in certain respects. On the other hand, it is a well-known fact that civilized women, especially of European stock prefer men of the Don—well—do not incline very much to the St. Anthony type. Civilized woman is far more sexually conscious than primitive woman. Women, primitive or civilized, are naturally immodest. Modesty, or what passes for it, has been forced on them by man because sex interferes with business. Women are forever fighting this restraint. Were it not for the law the standard of modesty among American and European women would be far below what it is. The tendency is toward boldness in dress and conversation. Among many African tribes before a girl can get a husband she must prove chastity before a jury of married women. Among other tribes infibulation is practised. In certain parts of Africa the unchaste bride is punished in a devilishly appropriate manner as Havelock Ellis tells. I know personally of one rite the natives of Sierra Leone used to practise until prevented by the British that showed the high value these people placed on chastity—I mean market value; for in Africa wives are generally purchased, just as among ourselves. We, however, are rather skilful at deluding ourselves to the contrary. Again, Shakespeare when he depicted woman's sexual character in his 'Sonnets to Sundry Notes of Music, IV,' certainly wasn't thinking of Negro women. Nor were Weininger, Schopenhauer, Tolstoi, Ibsen, Strindberg, Bocaccio, Balzac or Maupassant when they wrote."

"In spite of all you may say to the contrary," persisted the senator, "the standard of morality among white women is infinitely higher than among Negro ones."

"I believe that a greater percentage of white women maintain their so-called honor than Negro ones because, as a group, the former are more cultured. On the other hand, it is precisely because of this, that the white women are more sex-conscious, and are thus more prone to sapphism, tribadism and those many other forms of sexual perversion studied by Ellis, Kisch, Kraft-

FROM "SUPERMAN" TO MAN

Ebbing, Bloch and others. In other words, colored women are less discriminating but more normal. It is most important to remember that it is almost impossible to repress the sex instinct. When repressed in one direction it merely crops out in another. No other people, however, are so skilful at deluding themselves that they have subdued these forces as the English-speaking ones. I do not speak however in condonation of the Negro woman who gives herself to white men. She is chiefly responsible for the low esteem in which the Negro group is held. She is responsible for the bastardizing of the race, and she cannot plead physical bondage any more. Nor is this illicit relationship confined to the ignorant and lower classes of colored women. Far from it. Let me add in passing that one great menace to the morals of colored women is the white installment collectors, insurance men, gas-men and others who stream into Negro homes when the men are at work. But the statement that all Negro women are immoral—one, that I hear very frequently on these cars, only on my last trip one of the directors of an insurance company made it to me—can mean only one of two things:—either it is a case where "all looks yellow to the jaundiced eye,' or the speakers have been associating with a class of colored women, as immoral and low as themselves and formed their opinions there, in which case their remarks apply with equal force to themselves.

"Looking at the matter factually the United States Census seems to bear out what I have just said. The latest figures available, that of 1923, give a higher percentage of white women found guilty of imorality, than of Negro women. The report on Prisoners, 1923, page 68, gives eight offenses in which native American women led both the Negro women and the foreign-born white women, one of which was, "Fornication and prostitution . . . keeping house of ill-fame . . . and adultery."

"You cannot separate Negro immorality from white immorality. The lives of both groups of citizens are inextricably woven together, I am convinced, that any attempt at improving Negro morals, to be effective, must be accompanied by a reform in the morals of the whites."

The train stopped and Dixon left to open the trap-door. In his absence the senator again diligently revolved in his mind all the conventional points of alleged Negro inferiority. At last he

FROM "SUPERMAN" TO MAN

decided that he had found one—a trait he felt sure the whites never had. Now, certain of victory, he waited for Dixon's return. Once, when the latter returned to the smoker to place towels for the new arrivals, he started to speak of it, but Dixon asked to be excused, saying that he had to see the newcomers to bed. Fifteen minutes later he returned and the senator said impressively:

"I have a point that conclusively proves Negro inferiority. The black man and the black man alone, is guilty of the most repulsive, most debasing practice known to humanity—a thing done by only the lowest of the lower animals, namely, the eating of their own kind. Even in this country you can find Negroes whose fathers and mothers were cannibals, since it was not until 1850 that the importation of Africans to these shores actually ceased. And the whole pack of those now here would be cannibals still if we hadn't dragged them away from their mess of human flesh. The white man has never been guilty of such a thing, not so far as we can trace our history, thank God!"

Dixon seemed unimpressed. He said quietly: "It is probably true that cannibalism still exists in parts of Africa as well as among certain Indian tribes in the wilds of Brazil, as reported by the Rice expedition. These primitives, however, do not view the matter in the same light as we. May I read you what Finot has to say on the subject?" The senator did not reply, but Dixon found the place and read:

"'If a mother passes through a village with a little one, all the others will go to her and take the child, hold it in their arms and make it jump. A cannibal who has just enjoyed a piece of human flesh is quite as capable of doing this as the most sensitive of our civilized folk. Cannibalism, itself, does not there present to these people the repulsive aspects that affect us, and to which we object so strenuously.'"

Dixon closed the book and said: "Contrary to your assertions, however, branches of the white race have been cannibals. Herodotus says that the Scythian soldier, vampire-like, used to suck out the blood from the first enemy he killed. The Padeans, he said, used to eat their dead while the Issedonians would kill and eat all those who very very ill or approached senility. The Huns used to drink human blood out of the

FROM "SUPERMAN" TO MAN

skulls of their enemy. Gibbon tells of the cannibalism practised by the hordes of Attila. Cannibalism existed in the British Isles as late as the 4th Century A. D. St. Jerome says—

" 'When I was a boy in Gaul I beheld the Scots, a people living in Britain, eating human flesh, and although there were plenty of cattle and sheep at their disposal, they would prefer a ham of the herdsman or a slice of female breast."

"This observation of St. Jerome is confirmed by the Welsh Triads. These documents accuse the Angles and Saxons of the practise. They say that cannibalism was openly practised at the court of King Ethelfrith. They also tell of the great fondness of one Giori, a Welshman, for human flesh.

"Furthermore, cannibalism existed in Perthshire, Scotland, in the 13th Century. It was also openly practised in Germany in 1648, after the Thirty Years War. Children, nuns, and old people, were caught and eaten. You'll find that in Hertz' 'Race and Civilization,' page 56. Too, reports from Russia in 1920 persisted that, owing to famine, people were eating one another. I could tell you a great deal more but I have said enough to show that cannibalism among black or white is rather a matter of time and conditions than of people or place. Cannibalism has been common to all mankind. The roasting alive of human beings in the South is but a relic of cannibalism, and one can well imagine those ghouls eating the flesh of the burnt Negro, in time of famine, in pretty much the same manner that the priests used to eat the burnt sacrifice. So far as this matter of cannibalism is concerned I do think that the men who grind out the lives of their fellows in sweat shops and live on the proceeds or go to Palm Beach and Monte Carlo to enjoy themselves are just as effectively eaters of human flesh as the African who eats the enemy he has slain in battle—and certainly less merciful."

The senator appeared more embarrassed than ever. Then suddenly another point had come to him. He felt sure that Dixon positively could not rebut this. He said, triumphantly, "What of the disagreeable odor of the Negro? I have known some of the Southern ladies to faint from this smell that finds an equal only in the skunk."

FROM "SUPERMAN" TO MAN

Dixon smiled inwardly. Was this man's prejudice so strong
that it affected even his sense of smell? he asked himself. There
flashed into his mind visions of full page ads in the leading
Sunday newspapers and popular periodicals, as well as street
car ads, recommending preparations to white people to remove
their odors. Many other details crowded into his mind as the
odor of shop-girls in heated department stores; of crowded
whites in the New York subways; of that of even cleanly, refined
white women and girls in thin shirtwaists, particularly when
excited; and of the deodorants used on the sleeping-car by passengers to drown their various odors. He mentioned none of
these facts, however, but said instead:—"May I read you what
Sir Harry Johnston has to say on this?" He took out his notebook and read the following quotation from "The Negro in the
New World":

" 'A striking peculiarity of the African is the musky, goat-like smell
exhaled from the sweat, more especially the axillary glands. The
odor is markedly characteristic of the African (it has not hitherto
been recorded among Asiatic Negroes) but also occurs to a much
slighter degree among the Europeans as an exhalation from the armpits. Yet, I would make bold to say, that this skin odor is not so dis-
gusting as that which comes from heated and unwashed Europeans
and Asiatics. It is practically absent from many Africans who keep
their bodies washed and clean. While in the United States I mixed
with Negro crowds and scarcely noticed any disagreeable smell, for
the Negroes, like the American whites are an inherently cleanly
people. I only detected the presence of disagreeable body odors coming from the offensively dirty Chinese travelling in public conveyances
or from newly arrived immigrants in New York.'

"Finot says:—'For a long time it was thought that white
men were exempt from this smell but now we have to admit
a strong smell peculiar to white skins—a smell that the
Japanese declare to be insupportable.'
"I'll tell you an experience of my own," continued Dixon.
"One day I entered the Chicago Art Institute after closing
hours. As I entered I was assailed by an odor that reminded
me strongly of Negroes loading banana boats at Port Antonio,
in the West Indies. Tracking down this pungent odor I found
it came from one of the scrub-women, who was not a Negro,
but a Pole. It was undoubtedly an odor of this sort that Huysman,

FROM "SUPERMAN" TO MAN

the great French novelist, described in 'Le Gousset,' when, in speaking of the odor from the armpits of French women working in the fields, he says: "It was excessively terrible; it stung your nostrils like an unstoppered bottle of alkali, it seized you, irritating your mucous membrane with a rough odor."

Silence. The senator lit up another cigarette. Dixon looked at the ceiling where the flies were dancing around the lights, then he smiled and said, "You said, sir, that you have known Southern ladies to faint from the odor of Negroes, suppose I tell you that African ladies also faint from the odor of white people!"

"Ridiculous! Impossible! I would never believe that."

"Well, we have the authority of Professor Arnold J. Toynbee of London University, who is said to be the greatest living historian. Dixon found a passage in his notebook and read:

"It is not only the Japanese who are upset by the white race's smell. A highly cultivated and fastidious lady of my acquaintance once went to stay for several months in South Africa and engaged a staff of native servants among them a little Kaffir maid. It happened several times that the maid on being summoned into the employer's presence fell into a sudden faint and the lady who was kind-hearted felt some concern. What could the matter be with the girl? Was it heart disease? Or was it just acute nervousness at finding herself tete-a-tete with a member of the "superior race?" The lady questioned the other servants only to have her questions parried and eluded in the usual provoking fashion. But at last an older servant who saw that her mistress was becoming really upset and, alarmed, succeeded in conquering her own reserve and embarrassment. "You needn't worry, Madam," she assured my friend, "there is nothing serious the matter with the girl. The fact is she has come straight from her village to you. This is her first place in white people's service and she isn't yet quite used to the white people's smell. But don't you worry. She will get used to it soon enough. Why look at us! We all used to faint at first, but now we have got over it. It will be the same for her, you'll see."

"You'll find that sir, on pages 231-232, of his "Study of History," Vol. I, London, 1934. In Africa, I also saw Negroes holding their noses at the approach of white people."

Silence for a few minutes broken only by the rattling of the train. Dixon, in spite of his endeavor to suppress it had the buoyant air of a winner. The senator appeared worried and ill

FROM "SUPERMAN" TO MAN

at ease. He apparently could think of no effective retort for he began to cavil "A few minutes ago," he objected, "you said— 'Caucasian blood, figuratively speaking.' What do you mean? The next thing, you'll be telling me is that there is no difference between that and Negro blood."

"There is neither Caucasian nor any other kind of blood— just human blood. May I read you what Finot has to say on this matter?" He had just found the place and was about to begin reading when both men started nervously from their seats.

"What's that," demanded the senator.

A noise like that of a barking dog was coming from the body of the car.

"Someone having a nightmare, I should say," laughed Dixon. "One hears some strange noises on a sleeping car at night."

"Cant be," said the other gruffly. "That's a dog."

Dixon went in to investigate. Soon, he returned, smiling. "You were right, sir. It was a dog. A lady had a poodle in her basket. In making down the beds, I pushed the basket up against the steam-pipes. The poor little fellow was being roasted alive, and he was trying to tell us about it. Lucky for him that he had a bark, and not like the barkless African dog, who got trapped in the hold of a ship coming from Africa and had to go three weeks without food simply because he could tell no one where he was."

Dixon, eager to change the conversation, went on to tell of passengers who walked in their sleep, and of how one nearly stepped off a moving train. But the senator seemed little interested in the incident and again brought up the original conversation. Dixon remembered the passage he had started to read, found it again:

" 'The anthropologists have not succeeded in finding the essential variations in the composition of the blood between men of yellow, black and white colors, of broad and narrow skulls, of the smallest cranial capacity and those of most astonishing greatness. What is no less conclusive is that the part which the composition of the blood plays in demonstrating the differences between races and species is known. It is only the blood of beings belonging to the same variety and the same species which may be injected into them with impunity. Thus the blood of a hare may be injected into the organism of a rabbit or that of a mouse into a rat, but the blood of a man may not

FROM "SUPERMAN" TO MAN

be injected into the organism of a dog, horse or any other animal. Neither can the blood of an animal be injected into the veins of a man. In all these cases the foreign blood will be destroyed or destroy the organism that receives the injection. On the other hand, the blood of a black man may be injected into the blood of a white or yellow. It goes without saying that the form of the skull as well as the other grounds on which the anthropological divisions rest, plays as negative a part as the color of the skin.'"

Dixon found another place and read:

" 'The oldest of all human classifications (color), is at the same time one of the most defective. Its errors are obvious the moment the specific characteristics of each of the categories are considered. For, while among those listed as white there are men whose skins are as black as ebony, the Bicharis or the Black Moors of Senegal, there are among the blacks, fair or yellow skins like the Bushmen. Whence is this difference of color? The skin of the Negro, the yellow man and the white is identical as to that which concerns its composition, the derm, the mucous membrane and the epidermis. What varies is the color of the cells of the mucous membrane; these are blackish brown in the Negro, pale yellow in the fair white, a yellow, more or less, in the brown whites. But when this difference of coloring is examined closely, it must be acknowledged that the milieu represented in particular in this case by the intensity of the solar rays, exercises a preponderant influence on it.'

"I have also a quotation from Von Luschan, professor of Anthropology in the University of Berlin, on this matter of color, from his address at the Universal Races Congress:

" 'Still weaker and more objectionable is the division as to color. We know now that color of skin and hair are only the effect of environment and that we are fair because our ancestors lived for thousands of years in sunless, foggy countries. Fairness is nothing else but lack of pigment and our ancestors lost part of theirs because they had no use for it.'

"Schopenhauer in 'The World as Will and Idea' says:

" 'There is no such thing as a white race, much as this is talked of, but every white man is a faded or bleached one!' "

He added, "I do not know whether you have observed it, sir, but there is a great similarity between the varieties in man and dog. There are dogs with white skins and silky hair; with black skins and woolly hair; with long noses and snub noses;

FROM "SUPERMAN" TO MAN

with round heads and long heads; with high cheek bones and ordinary ones, just as among black men and white men. There is also a suspicious resemblance between the color of Caucasians and just plain pork, a food condemned by Mohammedans, Jews and Zulus. Indeed, very few Caucasian beauties can equal in complexion the rosy, dainty freshness of a newly shaved sucking-pig."

The senator was listening attentively and said nothing, Dixon resumed his reading:—

"'Very frequently the so-called inferior races show precisely the physiological properties, which, by revising all preconceived methods, place them at the head of humanity. After stating that superior races are furthest removed from the anthropoid apes, whilst inferior races are nearest to them, they bring together all the facts which in this respect favor the whites and entirely forget those in which Negroes are shown to be favored. . . .

'In the blood of modern Europeans flows that of Negroes, who lived on the continent at the end of the Quaternary epoch. . . .

"Let us remember that according to Giuseppe Sergi, Professor Brinton, and others, the white race, the ethnological pride of Europe, is only the direct fruit of a Negro race, the Eurafricans established in Europe from time immemorial and who came from North Africa. . . .' "

"But what of the skull of the Negro," objected the senator. "The brain of the black is much smaller than that of the white. The complexity of the convolutions of the Negro's brain is also far less intricate. It is not unlike that of an orang-outang. The sutures of the Negro's skull also close much earlier than the white man's and thus prevent the growth of the brain."

"The so-called science of craniometry or head measurement," replied Dixon, "as a means of determining mentality, has been discredited even by the third-rate scientists, it having been thoroughly exploded for some time. Burt G. Wilder, once president of Cornell University, in an essay on 'The Brain of the American Negro,' after a most careful examination of all the arguments, shows how thoroughly ridiculous is such a theory. So has Professor Ripley of the Massachusetts Institute of Technology in his book 'The Races of Europe.' "

Dixon continued his reading from Finot:—

"'All these measurements with their imposing numbers and scientific pretensions, as also the theoretic observations, resolve themselves

FROM "SUPERMAN" TO MAN

as we have seen into a nebulous doctrine which affirms many things
and proves nothing. The exact instruments which anthropologists
and craniometrists use offer a fantastic data. The results of their
operations are deposited in thousands of volumes, and yet, what is
the real meaning? In examining them closely one can hardly attribute
to them a descriptive value, so much do they contradict and destroy
each other.' "

Dixon began to look for another passage he was desirous of
reading, saying in the meanwhile, "In this passage note the
difference between the voices of Science and Prejudice:

" 'An analysis of all the theories on inequality created in us before
everything else a profound astonishment at the inertness of our
thought. When we go through the list of external differences which
appear to divide them, we find literally nothing which authorizes their
division into superior and inferior beings. The science of inequality
is emphatically a science of white people. It is they who have invented it, and set it going, who have maintained, cherished, and
propagated it, thanks to their observations and their deductions.
Deeming themselves greater than men of other colors, they have elevated into superior qualities all the traits which are peculiar to
themselves, commencing with the whiteness of the skin and the pliancy
of the hair. But nothing proves that these vaunted traits are traits
of racial superiority. Human varieties have not been studied like
those of animals and plants without conventional prejudices to their
respective values and as to those which are superior and inferior.
Facts have often yielded to sentiments. We have often been per-
suaded with the help of our feelings to accept our own preferences
rather than impartial observations, and to our own prejudices rather
than scientific laws. The purity of the blood which we create at will
becomes impossible in humanity. The Negroes are related to the
Whites who are linked to the Yellows as these last have common
links with both Negroes and Whites.' "

Dixon closed the book and said: "It is highly illogical to
assert superiority because of any physical trait whatsoever.
There is no physical human quality that cannot be found in a
superior form among the lower animals and even the plants
and the minerals. Do not poets and lovers when they wish to
speak enrapturedly of parts of the human body compare them to
gazelles, swans, dogs, lilies, snow, pearls, the dawn?"

The senator started to reply. Just then the train conductor
entered and asked Dixon for the tickets of the passengers who

had got on at the last station. Asking to be excused he left the room with the conductor.

Soon afterward the senator retired to his drawing-room, but this ruthless shattering of his pet theories forbade sleep. He was in a blind rage and with himself most of all. Why had he started to argue with this menial? The idea of a Negro, a common Negro porter, a member of a race he so thoroughly despised possessing enough knowledge to beat him in an argument! His anger increased as he remembered the calm and polished bearing of the porter as contrasted with his own rude manner, he, a Caucasian and a United States senator. Worst of all, he had to acknowledge even to himself the logic of the porter's arguments backed up as they had been by such an array of the authorities of his own race. Of this Universal Races Congress, which seemed so important, he knew nothing. Of the science of anthropology, he had to confess also that he knew little. As points of the discussion kept revolving in his mind, particularly those relating to immorality and odor, his hatred for the whole Negro people welled up in his heart stronger than ever. Ah, but after all, there was some consolation! This man was only a Negro porter. No matter how much knowledge he possessed, he, as a white man was the better of the two. No matter what the real truth was the world recognized him as the better man. He had power, the Negro none. He could enter places where this Negro dared not, except as a menial. But deep in his heart was an involuntary admiration for his opponent.

SECOND DAY

"The man's body is sacred, and the woman's body is sacred,
No matter who it is—it is sacred—is it the meanest one in
  the laborer's gang?
Is it one of the dull-faced immigrants just landed on the
  wharf?
Each belongs here or anywhere just as much as the well-off,
  just as much as you.
Each has his or her place in the procession."

—Walt Whitman.

The senator slept late the next morning. On awaking better thoughts came to him. These were improved by Dixon's cheery and respectful salutation to which he responded in a shame-faced and somewhat gruff manner. Dixon, however, refused to notice this. All that day the senator noted Dixon's conduct, his unobtrusive manner, his solicitude for the women passengers, his gentleness with the children and his amiability toward all, and he began to like him in spite of himself. Yet, the thought of his defeat rankled within him and made him decide to seek another occasion to talk with Dixon in the hope of saving his face.

That night when Dixon again went to the smoker to read, he returned. Dixon was sitting in the chair this time and he rose. "Won't you have this chair, sir? I am sure you will find it more comfortable than the couch."

"No, thank you," refused the senator, a little abruptly, seating himself on the couch opposite, at the same time motioning Dixon to keep his seat. Taking out his cigarette case he passed it to Dixon, who smilingly refused.

"Reading again, I see," broached the senator after a few minute's silence.

"Ye-es."

"What is it now?"

Dixon foresaw a re-opening of the argument and decided to prevent it. Though passionately fond of debating he did not like arguments on the color question, especially with white persons. He had blamed himself very much for the happening of the night before and determined not to be caught again. When the senator entered he had been reading of Negro mentality, but just prior to that the subject had been the civilization of the ancient Celts. He replied:

"I was reading about the Druids," and without giving the other a chance to reply, he began to speak about the customs of these ancient Britons. Then he started to tell of the customs of some of the countries he had visited. Now and again the senator would make a remark designed to lead the conversation into the channel he desired but each time Dixon would side-step it. Once Dixon told of how in Damascus he saw a Syrian carrying a great many chickens to market all with their legs tied together and heads hanging down. The senator immediately seized upon that to speak about Negroes and chickens in the South. But Dixon steered clear of this by telling him of the ruins of Greece, Pompeii, the Colosseum, Guatemala, and the remains of the Cliff-Dwellers in New Mexico, Arizona and Utah. The senator, at that, pointed out that the Negro had no such monuments to his credit. Dixon told him of Nubia and Lybia, of the Sphinx, Zymbabwe, and the other ruined cities of Mashonaland, and was just beginning an account of a visit to the Ethiopian ruins at Meroe, when the other wedged in a remark about the Negro and the Indian and began to speak of the superiority of Indian mentality over that of the Negro. He concluded with— "The Indian did not submit to slavery while the Negro did. My great-grandmother was a Cherokee princess and I am proud of it. The Indian is superior to the Negro?"

Dixon did not reply for a few moments, then somewhat nettled by the last remark he said to himself with sudden decision, "You want me to argue the color question, do you? All right, I will, but don't blame me if I give it to you worse than last night. Aloud, he said:—

"The Indians were enslaved successively by the Spanish, French, English and Portuguese. There were Indian slaves from Canada to Florida. The decline of Indian slavery was due chiefly to its being an economic failure. The Indian could not stand the hardships, nor the whiskey, drugs, and diseases of the white man. Large numbers of them died from smallpox, consumption and syphilis. The Negro was introduced, supplanting both the Indian and the white, as a worker. A white slave was far more valuable than an Indian one, and a Negro more than either.

FROM "SUPERMAN" TO MAN

A Negro was reckoned as the equivalent of five or six Indians, and sometimes brought a price nine times as high. You can find some interesting reading on this in 'Studies in History, Economics and Public Law,' Columbia University, Vol. 54.

"There were Indian slaves in the remainder of the New World but they, too, died off whenever they came in contact with the whites. Take the island of Jamaica. Two hundred and fifty years after discovery, its aborigines, the Arawaks, had disappeared to a man while the Negro brought there as a slave and subjected to much harsher treatment is, today, virtual master of the island. I have seen a great deal of Indian life, principally in Montana, Nevada, Arizona and the Canadian North-West, and I say very frankly that I think it very much below the Negro standard. Today the Indians of the Eastern and Southern States, and notably of Oklahoma, are more Negro than anything else."

The senator again brought up the subject of Negro mentality and Dixon referred him to the following quotation from Professor Myers, lecturer on Experimental Psychology at the University of Cambridge, England, in his address to the Universal Races Congress:—

" 'The majority of the peasant class through Europe are essentially the same as those of primitive communities.' "

At this point, another passenger, on his way from the observation car, entered the room. Handing a telegram to Dixon, he asked him to send it at the next stop. When the passenger was gone the senator again brought up the same subject and Dixon read him the following from Finot:

" 'It is fruitless to maintain the theory of the mental inferiority of Negroes. Twenty years of intellectual work has often proved sufficient for a Maori, Zulu, Indian or Negro to win back in his individual self, the centuries of mental arrest or mental sleep experienced by his congeners. This property common to all human beings provides them at once with a trait of ineffaceable equality.

" 'The psychology of primitive peoples and especially of Negroes strangely resembles that of the uncultured classes of Europe. Their prepossessions, ideas, and superstititions betray a similarity which draws them singularly together. The inhabitants of Negro villages in Central Africa are like the peasants living far from railways in the extreme north of Russia, or the extreme south of Italy.' "

FROM "SUPERMAN" TO MAN

Dixon lowered the book and said:—"One of the greatest arguments advanced in support of alleged Negro inferiority,—an argument that not a few Negroes will admit—is that the Negro has been a slave. I am convinced, however, that if the slave traders had captured some primitive European people and subjected them to the same dehumanizing treatment the result would have been the same. The great amount of ignorance in Russia, today, is undoubtedly due to the fact that the Russians were slaves for centuries. In Richard Hildreth's 'Memoirs of Archie, a White Slave,' (a record of slavery in America), a prominent slave dealer says: (here Dixon consulted his notebook):

" 'Just catch a stray Irish or German girl and sell her—a thing sometimes done—and she turns a 'nigger' at once, and makes just as good a slave as if there were African blood in her veins.'

"The more I study sociology the stronger grows my belief that the difference between one human variety and another is solely the result of environment."

"But," objected the senator, "even in the black man's home the white man is master. Look how easy it is for small numbers of white men to rule millions of peoples of all the other races! Look at India! A mere handful of Anglo-Saxons holding in subjection nearly four hundred million natives. Then, too, take the New World! What was it before the white man came here? Imagine what it would be now if he had not come here! Look at China, the oldest civilization in the world! It stood still for thousands and thousands of years until the white man got there. Japan owes its progress to the white race. My race has conquered or over-run every country on the globe. My race rules, Europe, the whole of Africa, except one or two inconsequential spots; the far greater part of Asia, the entire New World and all Australia; in short it is master of the whole world. That all the world is a richer, healthier, better place to live in is due entirely to the magic touch of the white race."

"Yes," replied Dixon," but like the cow that gave the pail of milk and then kicked it over, the white race is doing its best to destroy all civilization. Two world wars in a quarter of a century is a record to contemplate!

FROM "SUPERMAN" TO MAN

"I will admit that the Caucasian branch of the human race is the most advanced industrially. It is the pioneering group today in nearly all lines, and will no doubt continue to be so for some time. I readily admit that world progress for the last six centuries, at least, is due almost wholly to 'white' initiative. But even this great energy is conquered by the climate and certain other conditions that have retarded the growth of most of these other peoples. The white man going to those countries with his superior weapons for taking life, his more high developed intellect, and keener predatory instincts, has a decided advantage over the natives. But he must be re-enforced from time to time by fresh numbers or he, too, is likely to yield to the spell of the environment. This is one of the principal reasons for the frequent shifting of colonial officials by the British Foreign Office. I have seen white men in the tropics sink so low as to be objects of disgust to the lowest native. Blackburn, speaking of this, says:—

" 'In Africa, the animalistic, self-indulgent white man approximates yet nearer the animal; the intellectually active, destitute of the stimulus of conversation and encounter with diverse opinions and nimble wits, becomes an intellectual fungoid.'

"One reason for this," added Dixon, "is the enormous amount of whiskey they swill in an effort to drown the monotony of tropical life.

"The white immigrant in the tropics becomes less energetic, while the black one in the northern latitudes improves in energy and acquisitiveness. The Negro, say in New York City, is much superior to the average white native of the tropics and most of our southern states."

"But Negroes have been living in northern latitudes for three hundred years, at least," protested the senator, "and yet from among them has not emerged one single genius; indeed not even one famous man. Many Negroes have acquired a pseudo-fame because of pampering by white admirers and gross exaggerations from their own race. Had they been white men they would have passed unnoticed in the crowd."

"It is true," acknowledged Dixon, "that the Negro has been living in these northern latitudes for a long time, but under

FROM "SUPERMAN" TO MAN

what debased conditions! Would whites have done any better think you? Look at the very large number of whites in Europe and America, who, to use a Rooseveltian phrase 'can hardly pull their own weight.' It is quite true, as you said, that the mediocre attainments of certain Negroes have been exaggerated because of their color, but is it not highly probable that since these men must have had inherent ability they would have done better but for the handicap of color? Thus, as you see, one balances the other. Since mediocrity is a human characteristic and is to be found among peoples having the widest and fullest opportunities for advancement, why marvel at its appearance in a people who have been almost universally and uniformly oppressed and repressed below the level of the lowest grade of self-respect?

"Yet there are many Negroes who have achieved national and international distinction, regardless of color. It is generally conceded that the most remarkable figure that the South has produced since Lincoln is Booker T. Washington. In my opinion he and Frederick Douglass are the two most remarkable figures the United States has produced. Both not only came from a lower depth than Lincoln, the most remarkable white man, but even when they achieved fame, they were always open to the attacks and insults of the lowest whites. Booker T. Washington was one of the greatest men of all time. The pages of Plutarch contain no more inspiring figure than Douglass.

There are also many Negro authors of unqualified merit, as Dunbar, Blyden, Casely Hayford, DuBois, Kelly Miller, Countee Cullen, W. S. Braithwaite and James Weldon Johnson. DuBois belongs to the aristocracy of English letters. There are few, if any, living English writers who excel him in eloquence and elegance of diction. Kelly Miller was an essayist of distinction; and Braithwaite is one of the leading critics of poetry in America. There are many other Negroes as George W. Carver, Benjamin Brawley, Carter G. Woodson, George S. Schuyler, Hubert Harrison, Monroe N. Work, H. O. Tanner, Granville Wood, William Pickens, William Grant Still, Paul Robeson, Marian Anderson, Roland Hayes, Richmond Barthe, C. C. Spaulding, Jesse Owens, and Joe Louis, who all measure up to national and international standards. If white America, with thousands of years of culture behind it and freer opportunities has produced

FROM "SUPERMAN" TO MAN

so remarkably few men of international standard—perhaps not more than half a dozen—how can you expect the recognized manifestations of genius from a people with the clank of the slave's chain still sounding in their ears? In two European countries, from a comparatively small number, men of Negro descent, Pushkin and Dumas, have led all the others in their respective spheres."

The wind was whistling through the ventilators, blowing in small flakes of snow. Dixon arose and closed the transom.

"But the ability of these men is due to their white blood," objected the senator when Dixon returned. "The pure-blooded Negro is absolutely incapable of reasoning. He learns like a parrot."

"It happens," replied Dixon, "that some of the men I just named like Miller, Harrison, Hayes, Carver and Pickens have no visible admixture of white strain. Harrison, who was the foremost Negro intellectual and lecturer, ranked in critical skill and accumulated knowledge with the very best among the whites. When I was in Europe I met and heard of several African lads fresh from the jungles, who were winning honors in the best universities there. An Oxford graduate told me of one James Chala Selfy, an old classmate of his, who, as a boy, was taken at random from among hundreds n a captured slave ship and carried to England. Selfy, he told me, eclipsed his classmates, particularly in Hebrew and Latin.

"Abbe Gregoire and Blumenbach speak of Amo, a full-blooded Negro who was an astronomer and a lecturer at the University of Wittenberg. A Zulu, T. Isake Seme, once won the gold medal for oratory at Columbia University. Negro novelists have been able to depict the sensations and emotions of the whites in a manner to satisfy the whites themselves. Shakespeare, when he created Othello with such stateliness and pride, taught that color had no effect on character. One of the ablest of all Othellos was Ira Aldridge, a Negro. He received honors from many of the European monarchs of his day. Bilal, an unmixed Negro, ranks next to Mohammed, who accorded him precedence in Heaven. Bilal was the first to utter the Azan, or Call to Prayer of the Mohammedans; Kafur was one of the most famous of the Mohammedan rulers of Egypt; Negroes have always played a prom-

FROM "SUPERMAN" TO MAN

inent part in Mohammedan affairs. Hannibal, great-grandfather of Pushkin, father of Russian literature, was a general in the army of Peter the Great; Magloire Pelage drove the British from Guadeloupe and commanded a brigade for Napoleon during the Peninsular war; Samory was called 'The Black Napoleon of the French Soudan'; and the story of Toussaint L'Overture is well-known. Sir Samuel Lewis and J. Thomas of Sierra Leone were also pure Negroes. I could name other full-blooded Negroes who have made good in Europe as the late Blaise Diagne, French Cabinet Minister, and Gratien Candace, who was head of the budget for the French Navy, one of the builders of the French merchant marine, and a Cabinet Minister.

"The founder of the first leading Negro newspaper, Robert S. Abbott, was an unmixed Negro, and so was Marcus Garvey who, so far, was able to rally the greatest number of Negroes around him. As Sir Harry Johnston said in 'The New Statesman':—'There is literally nothing in the way of education that the Negro cannot master and master rapidly.' In 1922, a full-blooded Negro, Rene Maran, won one of the chief literary prizes in that greatest of all literary centers, France."

The senator appeared to be in deep thought and made no reply. Dixon took up his book again and began to read. After a few minutes he said. "Here are some interesting facts from Finot relative to the progress of the Negro:

" 'In 1899 there were eight per thousand destitute among the Negroes. The whites show as many, but these last had sixty-four rich for one rich Negro. Of one hundred proprietors seventy-five were whites to twenty-five blacks, but proportionately the latter should not have been more than twelve or thirteen. Of one hundred Negro houses, eighty were free from mortgage while there were only seventy whites.' "

Dixon consulted his notebook and said, "The census of 1910 shows one pauper for every 1,053 whites; one for every 1,505 Negroes.

"This advance from almost nothing ought to silence the talk of color-superiority, an advance below par, it is true, when one considers the progress of the average European immigrant, but for the Negro really miraculous when one considers the double handicap under which he has to struggle.

FROM "SUPERMAN" TO MAN

"The Indian, in spite of the better treatment accorded him, wilts under the rigors of civilization. As Dr. Charles Eastman, the leading American Indian, said at the Races Congress, the American Indian has failed to meet this test. The Indian has decreased: the Negro has increased. If the theory of the survival of the fittest is the test of virility, the Negro ranks with the best. Indeed, that fortitude that brought him through two hundred and fifty years of a cruelty unparalleled in medieval or modern history; that tenacity that makes him hold on when the Indian quits; that spirit of independence which keeps him in lesser numbers from the poorhouse than the Caucasian with his thousand superior chances; that buoyancy that makes him smile even in the midst of persecution, would justify my saying he is the fittest of the fit.' "

The bell began to ring. Dixon asked to be excused, and went to answer the call. Returning to the smoker he drew a glass of water and took it to the body of the car. When he came back, the senator remarked with some hesitancy:—"The truth about the matter is that the Negro is uncouth. He has nothing of the finer feeling of the white man. Listen to a gathering of Negroes anywhere. It sounds like a hundred flocks of jays, or rather, crows—jim-crows. Listen to their plantation guffaws on the street-cars of Northern cities, riding among white people. You never see white people acting like that anywhere."

This reminded Dixon of a remark made by the senator that first afternoon in the smoker. "You can't tell me anything," he had said, "a 'nigger' is a nigger.' " It would have been a breech of sleeping-car ethics to have said anything then. Now he saw his chance. He remembered his resolve to tell the other what he considered a few plain truths, and remarked composedly: "There is a great deal of truth in what you say, sir, but does it apply to the Negro alone? The major part of all peoples are unpolished. Some whites, however, forget this. In setting a standard they pick out the cream of their own group and endow all the remainder with the qualities of this choice portion. Conversely, they pick out the worst among the Negroes and measure all by the conduct of the bad, insomuch that at the very mention of his name a Negro has already been weighed and found

FROM "SUPERMAN" TO MAN

wanting. One often hears it said of a good Negro: 'He is colored, but——' "

"But," interrupted the senator, 'Nig—Negroes look down on their people. They exhibit the highest contempt for their own kind and can't get along together when out of the white man's jurisdiction. To get the best out of them they must be supervised by white people."

"There is a great deal of truth in what you have just said," admitted Dixon, "A good many Negroes are harsher to their own people than are many whites. A good many, as you say, have the greatest contempt for their own and would much sooner patronize a business conducted by a white person than one of their own even when the service is inferior. The fact is that I generally meet a higher grade of courtesy and consideration among the whites than among my own people, but usually only when I am content to occupy a menial position. The average Negro does need a greater respect for his own people. He is not unique in this respect, however. I have met many Jews and a few Irish who look down on their own people. One of the greatest anti-Semites I have ever met turned out to be a Jew himself. Karl Marx, a Jew, was one of the worst anti-Semites, and Hitler could not fail to learn hatred of the Jew from what Marx wrote about Jews. This is one of the traits of peoples who have been forced together, good and bad, very much, I suppose. Depreciate any name and certain of its possessors will always try to escape it. As you may recall, Thomas Buckle tells how the Scotch members when they first entered the British Parliament, tried to ape the ways of the English members, and were generally ashamed of things Scotch. Some of Dr. Johnson's best jokes were made on the alleged inferiority of the Scotch. But, as I was going to say, the majority of the whites even in this country, are mediocre. This class, accomplishing nothing beyond the powers of a similar class in any race, most arrogantly plumes itself upon the accomplishment of the highest class of whites, its arrogance and easy assumption of superiority increasing in proportion to its inability. But I do not blame them very much. They merely reflect in their coarse way the actions and sentiments of a very large number of educated and supposedly refined whites. I can't see any difference, whatever,

FROM "SUPERMAN" TO MAN

between the spirit of the scavenger who objects to working with a Negro, and that of a Princeton or Vassar student who objects to one in the class-room, or a Daughter of the American Revolution who objects to letting a Negro singer of international fame sing in Constitutional Hall.

"You also justly remarked that certain Negroes were loud and uncouth. This also happens by the way to be the same opinion that many Europeans hold of some of the American visitors to Europe. In the tourist season one can see parties of American tourists, Baedekers in hand, in the Louvre, the Schonbrunn, or Unter Den Linden, all chattering at the top of their shrill piercing voices with their, 'Hey, sis, lookee yere' or some such exclamation. They will even enter cathedrals where persons are at worship, still chattering loudly. Their loud laughter on tramways and omnibuses is just as disagreeable to Europeans, from what I have heard them say, as is that of certain Negroes and whites of the lower classes to the more cultured here in America, regardless of color."

Dixon could see from the flush on the other's face that he was not relishing the turn the conversation had taken, yet he felt is his duty to tell this other side of the story. He took advantage of the other's silence to continue:—"The general attitude of white Americans towards the Negro,—I except those who treat him fairly—is that of a man who is doing his best to prevent his pet theory being proved wrong. The doctrine of Negro inferiority has been preached for a long time. Now that the Negro's progress has proved it quite false, everything that can be done is being done to prevent the truth from coming out. This, at any rate, seems to be the case, for the usual way is to give one a trial and then, if he fails, accuse him of inferiority. But to accuse him in advance is—well—to show fear of being proved wrong."

As the senator was not replying, Dixon decided to end the conversation by introducing another subject. After a short pause he inquired:—"You have been out West before, haven't you, sir?' But the senator evidently did not intend to abandon the subject, for after an absent-minded, "Yes," he resumed—"You spoke a little while ago of the arrogance of the lower class white men. I can think of no more arrogant being than a Negro in authority. I have met Negro porters and Negro elevator men who acted as if they owned the earth." He went on to tell some of his experiences.

"I happen to know many such myself," confirmed Dixon, warmly. "Many Negroes do not care to work under bosses of their own group, because of the severity and exactions of many of them. During slavery as you know, the most brutal slave-drivers came from among the slaves. In the West Indies, Negro slave-drivers were specially chosen for the white slaves. This trait, I fear, is still with many of us. White 'straw-bosses,' by the way, are just as ignorant and imperious, as we, railroad men, and former soldiers know only too well. Persons like these, black and white, suffer from an inferiority complex and badly need lessons in, what to me, represents the only real superiority—courteous conduct and respect for human personality."

Dixon remembered the other's conduct that first afternoon in the smoker and he continued in even, impersonal tones: "My idea of a superior man is one who has, first of all, an instinctive consideration for the feelings of others. Such a one does not vulgarly or otherwise, assert his color or his social position. He would no sooner brag about his race than about himself, seeing that both these offenses against good taste are, at bottom, the same. However much a really cultured person might see his superiority to others, he will not mention it, nor compliment himself too much. It is no uncommon thing to hear persons expressing their idea of their own importance by speaking contemptuously of their fellow-men in such terms as 'dagos,' 'sheenies,' 'wops,' 'niggers,' 'coons,' 'poor white trash.' One never hears white men like Edison, Einstein, Carrel, Wendell Willkie, Norman Thomas, Henry Ford, Rockefeller, Franklin D. Roosevent, and those who are busy doing something really big bragging about their race. They leave that to the other fellows, who find in it a compensation for their own littleness. The mere fact of a man's proclaiming his superiority is, in itself, an indication that he feels it cannot speak for itself. 'Don't tell me who you are,' said Emerson, 'what you are speaks so loud, I can't hear you.' "

Dixon saw that the senator had taken his remarks personally, as he had intended he should. He felt his opponent really needed the lesson, and continued in a polite but impressive tone:——

"It strikes me that the one great thing White America has yet to decide—again I except those who practise justice—is this: Is the Negro a human being, or is he a creature somewhere between man and monkey? Is he an American citizen or isn't he? He is legislated against, and everything that will help destroy his self-respect is done. In every part of this country from the Great Lakes to the Rio Grande, except in parts of Maine and Vermont, he is in some way or other made to feel lower than the most objectionable alien. Indeed, the Negro is the only one treated as an objectionable alien in this country. And the irony of it all is that he is expected to smile and be pleasant always."

He added reflectively: "But he is going to stop smiling some of these days and settle down to serious thought. Already some of these laughing ones are like Victor Hugo's Laughing Man whose face of constant laughter hid a heart full of bitterness."

Dixon could see that the senator was getting angrier, but he continued: "Very often on these cars and in other public places white men will say the most scurrilous things possible, altogether disregarding my presence. Especially do they delight in speaking, even boasting to me of their amours with Negro women in the lewdest language. Usually these are the very ones who are most sensitive about the women of their own race. Chicken-stealing, too, according to the jokesmiths, seems to be the principal occupation of Negroes. Very many whites seem unable to imagine a Negro, however decent, as being anything else but a minstrel, and jokes like these are supposed to portray the full depth of Negro character, cultured and uncultured. It seems that the desire of such is to degrade the highest Negroes to the level of the lowest in the mass. This makes me reflect, not a little, on this matter of superiority: for since truth is the most superior thing in all the world, it is clear that we are superior to others only in proportion as we exceed them in living up to the truth. I refer particularly to the ability to recognize good qualities in others not belonging to our own race, class or sect."

The senator rose excitedly. This lecturing, this presumption on the part of a Negro, was more than he could stand. He started

FROM "SUPERMAN" TO MAN

for the doorway, but his pride drew him back when half-way.
No, he could not run away and leave the Negro master of the
field much as the situation exasperated him. He began pacing
the room, his body swaying with the motion of the train. Then
he asked himself why should he be angry. It was he who had
started the discussion, and the Negro, at no time, had been disre-
spectful. Indeed, he felt a sort of fascination for the frank and
courteous bearing of the man. This porter, he knew, was telling
the truth. Why, he asked himself, should he be angry at hearing
the truth? In the analysis many points between right and policy
in the treatment of the Negro dawned upon him. The more
concretely he saw the matter, the less he liked his stand. In this
thoughtful vein he resumed his seat, lit another cigarette and
relapsed into thought. After a few minutes, he demanded, "Am
I to assume then that prejudice against the Negro is a distinc-
tively American trait?"

"No," said Dixon, "the British have it, too, as well as most
colonial whites. You'll find it very active in the Dominion of
South Africa, especially in the former Boer republics, in that part
of Canada inhabited by Anglo-Saxons; in parts of British West
Africa, and to a certain extent in Cuba and the British West
Indies. Color egotism, is, however, peculiarly American in this:
In none of the places mentioned does it ever extend to lynching
and burning alive, not even in the Transvaal or Orange River
Colony, where the dislike is perhaps even stronger than in the
South. In all of these countries intelligence and self-respect,
in no matter whom, is respected. Cultured Negroes suffer less
discrimination. It must be remember that the Negro in the
United States is far ahead of the South African one. The percentage of illiteracy among the Negroes of Natal is not less than
sixty percent. The Negro in the United States, broadly speaking,
is ahead of the Negro everywhere else. In all of the countries I
have mentioned color prejudice is directed chiefly against the
ignorant Negro—an attitude none the less wrong. In the United
States, on the other hand, little, if any, distinction is made between good and bad, cultured and uncultured. Indeed, the refined Negro is often singled out as the especial object of attack,
while the lower class one—the 'Uncle Tom' kind—is more
popular, that kind being the one most idealized in white litera-

FROM "SUPERMAN" TO MAN

ture. From this, one may justly argue that in the United States we have color jealousy; not color prejudice; not contempt but fear; and that the situation is maintained by the whites as a smoke screen for their own defects. In Europe the stronghold of the white race, instead of finding color a bar, I more often found it an asset, while in the United States I have it everywhere thrust at me that I am not wanted. Even in remote Northern villages, like Merril, Wis., I have been refused food. As I travel over this country the greatest trouble I have is to have food served me. There are towns in the North as Sterling, Pa., or Tonowanda, N. Y., where the most self-respecting Negro is not permitted to pass a night; there are towns in Texas and the South where if I but step from the train to the ground I do so at the peril of my life. Yet we are Americans of the Americans. The 1930 census gave only 98,620 foreign-born Negroes, or less than one per cent. Our past is woven into the most intricate texture of the republic. Negroes in the service of the Spaniards were laying the foundations of the Southern States before Sir Walter Raleigh, the founder of Virginia, was born. They arrived in Virginia, in 1526, or twenty-six years before the birth of Raleigh. In 1536, or eighty-four years before the Pilgrim Fathers arrived, a Negro, Estevanico, made the first voyage across the American Continent, from Florida to California, and discovered Arizona and New Mexico. But while the descendants of the Pilgrims, and even of the whites, who arrived as slaves and convicts, constitute the nobility of America, we are still in the discard.

"This cannot be due to lack of accomplishment for we have done enormously more than the Indian, descent from whom any number of whites will boast of. The Spartan was not more unflinchingly loyal to his country than we are, yet even the but-yesterday-arrived alien, whom our forefathers and we have fought to make and to perpetuate this republic, have far more actual rights than we—solely because of the color of his skin. Although the Negro thinks in pretty much the same channels and has generally the same habits, class for class as the whites, not to speak of blood relationship, the attitude is to speak of all Negroes as if they had just come from Africa. Baron d'Estournelles de Constant of the French Senate is undoubtedly right

FROM "SUPERMAN" TO MAN

when he says in his book on this country: 'The Negro is a freedman not a citizen.' "

"But the Negroes in the South American countries and the West Indies belonged to a higher type of African," replied the senator." The most peaceful ones were taken to those countries, while the most cannibalistic were brought to us."

"You will find in reading the history of the West Indies that the slaveholders there made a reverse complaint with far juster cause. A general massacre of the whites like that at Cape Francois, Haiti, in 1791, was no uncommon occurrence. And after all why shouldn't a man be warlike in defense of his freedom?

"The Negro in every part of the world, I have noticed, is just what his treatment makes of him. In Brazil and Jamaica, I found him keenly conscious of his dignity as a man and a citizen. In the United States where numbers are against him and where he is compelled to slink, as it were, through life, afraid to go into this or that place, wondering whether he will be served, he is naturally timid and inclined to be spiritless. Some years ago the head of one of the most famous educational institutions in the world, and his wife, were ejected from a sleeping-car on account of color. A similar incident would have happened nowhere else in the world except, perhaps, South Africa. Sir Charles Bruce with his vast colonial experience very rightly said at the Universal Races Congress that the American Negro had encountered at every stop of his progress 'the most formidable opposition that the forces of avarice, jealousy, hate and fear have been able to command.' While I have met many whites, who, in spite of their environment, are quite as unprejudiced as any European, I have noticed North, South, East and West, and particularly in the South, so general an exhibition of this feeling, ofttimes from those one would think above such petty conduct, that I have been forced to the conclusion that, far more often than not, a white skin in America is the livery of servitude to the most stupid and exacting of all tyrants—Czar Prejudice. These slaves are of varying degrees—from the fanatically devoted as the lyncher to the morally timid—those who will not speak to intimate Negro acquaintances on the street for fear of what others will think."

FROM "SUPERMAN" TO MAN

The senator did not reply. Dixon continued: "I doubt if one white person in a million of those who do not like Negroes could give himself one honest reason for his attitude. Lord Brougham spoke for such when he said: 'I never knew anyone to hate me but those whom I had served and those who had done me some great injustice.' The real cause can certainly not be one of color, or why is the European, who sees little of Negroes, not prejudiced against them? Why also the great amount of racial intermixture that has always gone on? Peoples from certain European countries come to this country in search of greater individual liberty, and find it, too; yet the Negro, an original citizen of the United States never knows how it feels to be a real man, until he goes to those countries whence these peoples came, as Russia, even when it was under the Czar. And what makes it harder to bear is that one hears so many effusions about liberty, democracy, and unlimited opportunies for all. When I returned to the United States, after I had been away for six years I landed at a Southern port. There, barred from the parks, libraries, and places of public amusement, I felt in this boasted land of freedom what the murderer of King Humbert of Italy must have experienced in his cell, the size of which did not permit him to stand upright or to lie at full length."

"But," objected the senator, "the South treats the Negro far better than the North. What do you notice after passing the Mason-Dixon line coming North? That nearly all the work done by black men in the South is done by white. In the South most of the manual labor is given them. We have a larger number of brakemen, locomotive engineers and other occupations from which they are barred by the unions in the North. They find ready employment in Southern factories, while they find great difficulty in getting into Northern ones. Then our unskilled labor is generally given to them. Janitors, porters, waiters and domestics are all Negroes. In the North these jobs are filled by white foreigners. The Southern white man is far more sympathetic to the Negro. We know his failings and make allowance for them; up here he is held to the same standard as the white man without the white man's chances. The black man knows he can always find a friend in us. Many have I helped, many have I saved from prison. Our cook has been with us thirty-eight

FROM "SUPERMAN" TO MAN

years. That man, white or black, that would hurt Aunt Hepsy would have to reckon with me first. No matter what you say you could never convince me that the North is a better place for your people than the South."

"I fear I cannot agree with you, sir," replied Dixon. "In the North Negro illiteracy is only 4.7 per cent; in the South it is 19.7. It is true that the Southerner is more sympathetic than the Northerner. As someone has said, the South likes the Negro as an individual, but detests him as a race while the North likes him as a race but detests him as an individual. It is true that Negroes find readier employment in the South, but this is due to necessity and color pride and not to altruism. As you know certain occupations as housework are considered below the dignity of white people in the South. Ray Stannard Baker tells of an instance where the chief argument used against the rapacity of the mob was that it was frightening the Negroes away, at cotton-picking time, leaving the job to be done by white men. This better opportunity for employment, in my opinion, is over-balanced by the greater freedom in the North. Man's great need is not paternalism, but freedom to develop initiative and independence and thus be self-respecting. The Northern policy helps to do this, thus making the Negro a greater asset to the nation. In the South, on the other hand, everything, it seems, is done to humble him and keep his spirit down. On a recent trip I was forced to pass two weeks in Louisiana and Alabama. The treatment I received there from the customs of the whites, after the freedom I enjoyed in Europe, made me feel as if I had stepped back into one of the darkest periods of human oppression. It was a great relief to return North again."

With an earnestness tinged with sarcasm, he continued: "Juvenal, Voltaire, Swift nor any of the great masters of satire ever had so pregnant and suggestive a theme as this color situation—this question of a pigmented or unpigmented skin, with or without straight hair, and the supposed significance of these to real manhood, in short, whether one's physical appearance is not a more reliable index to his mental and moral qualities than his psychic qualities. The doctrine of superiority as based on skin-color and and hair, would tell us that Shakespeare's physical body was superior to his mind. This crudest form of materialism, this profoundest ignorance of which the mind is capable—thrives in our universities and courts of law.

"In this tragic farce there are a thousand and one idiosyncrasies. For instance, a Negro chauffeur or janitor with his family will be permitted to live in the most aristocratic neighborhood, but if either of them was to become a professional and live as an independent citizen in that same neighborhood there would be a storm of protest. Though a paragon in character, he would be likely to have his house bombed or set on fire at midnight as was the case with a Negro artist at Oak Park, Ill.; a white man may live in undisturbed concubinage with a Negro woman, but let him attempt to live with her according to civilized ideals and the law will at once send him to prison as in cultured California and Indiana, and all the Southern States; a lady whose baby is being suckled by a Negro nurse and is waited on by a Negro porter will go into hysterics and sue for damages because another Negro is a passenger in the same car; a pugilist marries a woman in his own class and it becomes the sensation of the day, a large number of citizens, white and black, lose their heads, jim-crow and anti-marriage bills flood the legislatures of nearly every state, becoming a law in many; a proprietor will refuse me a sandwich in the business part of his lunch-room lest his doing so will make me the social equal of his patrons thus giving me the right to call upon them, unbidden, and court their daughters; a certain law will permit the most uncleanly Indian or Mexican in a car from which the cleanest, most refined Negro would be barred, or even a white person saying he had Negro blood. But the situation becomes tragic when it results in gross injustices like these—a white man taken in a Negro brothel is set free but the women are fined; a Negro found in a white brothel is sentenced to death, his sentence being commuted to life imprisonment. A Negro, Holinshed, catches his wife and her white lover in bed and kills them both. He is acquitted for killing the wife, but is sentenced to death for killing the lover. Voltaire spoke wisely when he said:—'Prejudice is the reason of fools.' It is possible that many of these persons are sincere, but what has education done for them?

FROM "SUPERMAN" TO MAN

Wherein do they differ from those primitive Africans who shun a white skin?"

Dixon had warmed up to his subject. He had spoken more heatedly than he had intended. He took up his book again. As he opened it the senator asked with ill-concealed sarcasm: "Am I to infer that you are in favor of social equality?"

"No, sir," replied Dixon with cheery decisiveness.

"But," queried the other, puzzled but mollified, "how is it possible for Negroes to stay at the same hotel and live in the same apartments as the white people and not have social equality! It is impossible for the races to have identical rights without social equality."

"Haven't white men equal rights, and yet not social equality?"

"You are always going off at a tangent," said the senator, irritably, "you clearly understood what I meant. Are you in favor of social equality? Yes or no?"

"No, as I said before."

"Why?"

"I always want the option of choosing my own company."

"What are you driving at?"

"It is so obvious that people will seek those they like and shun those they dislike that I couldn't help thinking that when you spoke of social equality you mean a forced association. Such an association would work both ways: unwelcome whites could force themselves upon Negroes who didn't want them, for instance. Equality, social or otherwise, has never existed and probably will never exist, not even among members of a secret fraternity."

"Well, you are too critical, anyway," said the senator, sharply, "what I mean is this:—do you or do you not believe that Negroes should meet white people in a social way—call upon them—pay them social visits in their homes?"

"Why! Both races have been doing that for—for the last three centuries, haven't they?" He added: "But like Nicodemus—by night!"

"Very well! Do you think that Negroes should be permitted to attend white dances and dinner-parties?"

"If such persons are friendly enough for that, why, certainly!

FROM "SUPERMAN" TO MAN

They meet in Europe among the same white race. Each of
the peoples in question can learn something ennobling from the
other, and ennobling influences have no color. When a Caucasian reads Terence, Esop, Dumas, Pushkin, Georgie Douglas
Johnson and Jesse Fauset; admires the paintings of Tanner, Scott
or Harper; or listens to the music of Coleridge-Taylor, Rosamond
Johnson, Dett or Burleigh, he associates with what for a better
name we will call Negro thought. If association with their
works, why not with the authors themselves?"

"But from the vast mass of Negroes the Anglo-Saxon has absolutely nothing to learn and if we let down the bars to a few
we'll have to let it down to the whole black flood."

"When you," retorted Dixon with considerable spirit, "merely
permit a citizen to enjoy his God-given rights does it mean that
you have to bring him to your home against your will, and perhaps his? No self-respecting white man will make social calls
uninvited. I, a Negro, would not for a moment think of in-
truding even in a Negro friend's home. This whole matter of
social equality revolves on the question:—Should a certain group
in this nation be permitted to regulate the intimate social affairs
of their neighbors, picking their acquaintances for them and
so on, as they do in Nazi Germany?"

He continued still more earnestly:—"But there is another and
yet more important phase of this question of so-called social
equality—the human side. The great-hearted man refuses to
imprison his soul behind bars of color, creed, or caste. In every
other he sees another human being fundamentally the same as
himself. Despite all barriers, he enjoys meeting kindred souls.
For him dignity, grandeur and nobility exist only in simplicity,
sincerity and sympathy. As even a leper convict can be exclusive
there is really nothing distinguished about the exclusive man."

"But the Negro doesn't want to mix with the whites. He
prefers to maintain his separate institutions. He is happiest
in his churches and schools by himself."

"That statement," returned Dixon, "is just the opposite of the
one you made a few minutes past. Then, you implied that
Negroes wanted what you called social equality now you say they
prefer segregation. What do you mean?"

FROM "SUPERMAN" TO MAN

"I mean just what I said—the mass of the race wants segregation."

"That," replied Dixon, "brings us back to our conversation about the universality of human nature. You will doubtless recall that the Tories did not want to be freed from George III. Most human beings will stomach anything provided they are half way comfortable. Things could be worse, they say. As the Declaration of Independence puts it:—'Mankind are more disposed to suffer while evils are sufferable than to right themselves by abolishing the forms to which they are accustomed.' This is especially true of Negroes. One hears frequently:—'Well, this is a white man's country,' or 'Well, you must remember you are colored.' Such still have the spirit of slavery. As for me, this is my country. My forefathers helped to make it what it is, and I am not going to be satisfied until I enjoy all the rights of a citizen. Did it ever strike you, sir, that the United States is the only country in the New World which has laws against its own citizens and give preference over them to certain aliens? There are no jim-crow laws for white and near-white aliens.

"As regards segregation, a great many Negroes do act as you say, but they cannot be wholly blamed since they are unwelcome in white places. Apart from this justifiable attitude, you will find a great many just as illiberal in this respect as the average white, perhaps more so. They cry for equal rights and segregation in the same breadth. I would wager that those Negroes who want segregation when they may have fuller rights are the direct descendants of that deputation of slaves who, according to Elbert Hubbard, waited on Lincoln and begged him not to sign the Emancipation Proclamation. But is the fact that some Negroes want segregation a justification for forcing it on those who don't?"

The senator did not reply. Dixon continued:—"And speaking of segregation, let spread-eagle orators rave as they may, the fact remains that in this Republic we have a caste system immeasurably more vicious than that of any European country, and, if you consider our superior educational advantages, worse than that of India. In Europe the lower classes are held in contempt by the upper, yet there are no segregation laws, except against

FROM "SUPERMAN" TO MAN

the Jews. Let me say in passing but not in defense of anti-Semites, that Jews, as a rule, wish to be exclusive, except in trade—a trait that is three thousand years old. The European peasant, if he has the push, may rise to the highest positions, Lloyd George, for instance. Imagine the most cultured and capable Negro in the Cabinet! Here in the United States this association of black and white is held repulsive. Not so in Europe, however. There the cultured non-white has entree to the most polished circles. Booker T. Washington was dined by Queen Victoria, the King of Denmark and other European rulers, but you recall the great fuss that was made when Theodore Roosevelt did the same. The French, undoubtedly, the most esthetic people on earth, welcome the Negro. Finot, speaking of the beauty of the American quadroon and octoroon, says: (here Dixon found the place):

" 'In France and in Europe all these women would be surrounded by the praises of men, whereas, in the Southern States they are penned in like lepers in special schools, special railway carriages, and special hotels.' "

"But——"

Just then the passenger with the nasal, drawing voice that had spoken to Dixon about the senator the first day, entered the smoker. After greeting the two he leaned against the washstand and with the freedom that exists on the trains began to listen to the conversation.

Dixon rose and offered him a chair.

"No, no; this is good enough for me," he said, seating himself near the senator, at the same time winking at Dixon and glancing at the former as if to say:—"I see he is at it again?"

Seeing that the conversation had suddenly ceased, he said aloud:—"I hope I am not interfering with your conversation."

"Not at all," said the senator. Turning to Dixon the newcomer urged—"Go on. Don't let me interrupt you."

Dixon hesitated but as the senator was looking expectantly at him, he continued:—"As I was going to say do not infer from my remarks that Negroes, generally, are hankering after social intermingling, either active or passive, with the whites. Few Negroes will attend such white functions at which they

FROM "SUPERMAN" TO MAN

would be welcome. For instance, Negroes are generally welcome at radical balls, yet few, even when personally invited and given complimentary tickets will attend. At a great Socialist ball in New York City recently there were only seven Negroes present, although there are thousands of Negro socialists and sympathisers in that city. One of the leaders said to me:—'Where are all the colored people? I thought they would be out on a night like this!' The same was largely true of the Communist ball. Negroes, as I said, are the original standpatters. All that the majority is asking is open competition in the labor market.

"Negroes have their own societies. I know many Negro families possessing all the charm and refinement of the best white families. Indeed, my protest is that most refined Negroes have all the herd respectability of white 'society.' They are white in everything but color. I also know individuals possessing as high ideals as are to be found in any white person I have met. But the average white knows as much of this home life among Negroes as he knows of the fourth dimension. Most of them meet only uneducated Negro porters and laborers, while others associate with the lower class of colored women and form their opinion of all from that type. This lack of knowledge is evident even in the writings of all but a few of those who write sympathetically on the color situation. There are also those who shut their eyes and ears resolutely to these things. Such are like those very devout persons who, although believing themselves firm in their own faith, steadfastly refuse to look into a doctrine in any way different from their own. But, ignore truth as we will, it creeps on like a mighty glacier, cold to claims of color, creed or clan, grinding to dust the mountains of falsehood. In whatever field the Negro has entered with the white man—in the university, in the professions, in the shop, or on the farm—he has held his own in spite of the handicaps of color. If this is not a superiority of the highest order the whole world needs to revise its idea of that word.

"The great majority of the Negroes of my acquaintance, so far as I can see, wish to preserve their social and racial identity. They do not ask social intermingling. In fact most of them are afraid of it. They feel out of place in white society, except as servants. All they want is to be able to come and go like the normal citizen of any country."

"That's what I say, too," added the newcomer heartily. "I stand for fair play to all. My experience is that if you treat a man right he will act rightly. If you treat him badly you will make him bad. The conduct of others towards us is usually the reflection of our own attitude toward them. I——"

"But social intermingling," protested the senator excitedly, "will lead to intermarriage. The Anglo-Saxon will never stand for the mongrelizing of his race. Better a thousand times that the whole race should be wiped out of existence first. The marriage of the black man to the white woman is an atrocity—a sin against the Holy Ghost." Turning to the newcomer, as if to enlist his sympathy, he added: "Our women must be protected. They must be protected if we have to kill off every other race. Whatever may be said of the white race no one can ever accuse it of ever failing to protect its women."

Dixon wondered whether the senator had ever read European history, or heard of the white woman's bitter struggle against white men for justice throughout the ages; of child labor, or of the low age of consent in the Southern States.

"That's where we agree," said the newcomer, quickly. "While I stand for fair play to the black man I strongly oppose intermarriage. The Negro is a far less developed race. It took the white man thousands of years to reach his present height, and until the Negro reaches that height the white man has everything to lose and nothing to gain by amalgamation. We must reckon on the effects of heredity. Another great objection to the marriage of a black man to a white woman is that except in rare instances he cannot provide for her as a white man could, and she must suffer. Yet, at the same time should you be unjust to a man simply because you wouldn't accept him as a son-in-law?"

Dixon had been expecting this phase of the color situation to crop up sooner or later and had prepared to meet it. He began: "There is a tendency among persons, otherwise calm, to get excited in discussing this phase of the color situation. The question is with us, and no amount of loud talking or agitation will alter that fact. It has been with us three hundred years and probably has a long time to stay yet. Why not look at it

FROM "SUPERMAN" TO MAN

calmly then, particularly as no one is being forced to marry against his or her will in the meantime? Getting excited never helps."

In calm, judicial tones, he continued: "Now, gentlemen, I find that this question of marriage between white and black resolves itself into seven principal points, as follows:—one against, four for the question taking care of itself, and two in favor of the proposition. I have honestly sought other adverse points as I wish rather to get at the truth than to prove a theory. I have failed to find any more, however. The point against intermarriage is that such unions are contrary to law in twenty-nine states, and well let us add—opposed in all the others by public opinion."

"Public opinion!" exclaimed the newcomer, eagerly, "there, you have said it! The voice of the people is the voice of God!"

"Very true, sir," said Dixon, softly, "the voice of the people is the voice of God, but only when it is instructed, when like the voice of God is expresses truth."

The passenger did not respond. Dixon continued:—"Now let us examine the others. First like the—"

He was interrupted by the entrance of another passenger, the travelling companion of the one that had entered a few minutes before. The two had been riding in the observation car. The last newcomer had stopped to talk with a brakeman, and No. 1 had preceded him. Dixon got up and offered him the chair, but he, too, refused it. After leaning against the dental lavatory for a few seconds he sat down on the couch between the senator and passenger No. 1.

These two looked at Dixon, expecting him to continue. As he did not No. 1 asked him to name his arguments in favor of intermarriage, at the same time explaining the circumstances to passenger No. 2. Upon the latter's allowing his interest in the matter, Dixon continued:—"As I was saying, first, like the Negro-hater, we will go to the Bible. Is such a marriage wrong theologically? Evidently not, for the Bible says that God struck Miriam with leprosy for objecting to Moses' Ethiopian wife, and Joseph and Solomon both married Egyptians. Of course, both Moses and Solomon were probably Negroes, still there is a

FROM "SUPERMAN" TO MAN

strong question of intermarriage even among some African tribes.

"Second, is it harmful biologically? Answer': It is possible to produce healthy offspring by a union of the most cultured type and the lowest of the most primitive. Some of the finest types, mentally and physically, have been produced by crossing dissimilar races as Coleridge-Taylor, one of England's greatest musicians; Lemuel Haynes, Frederick Douglass, Booker T. Washington, and General Dumas.

"Third, is it wrong ethically? Quite the contrary. Our laws forbid sexual immorality. Here is where the law is in conflict with itself. Bryce, in his 'American Commonwealth,' speaking of the law forbidding the marriage of black and white, says it is 'one of the least defensible of all laws.' Fourth, the right to select one's mate is one of the most ancient, most sacred of individual rights, and when the state interferes in this, except in the case of the mentally unfit, it but adds humor to the witticism—'This is a free country.' "

The rattle of a freight train in the opposite direction made it impossible for Dixon to continue. When the noise was over the three looked at him to go on.

"The two reasons in favor of intermarriage," he went on, "are first, it is beneficial, sociologically. As the color of the mulatto is generally more pleasing not only to the whites but to the blacks, the situation is improved. Theodore Roosevelt, in an article on Brazil in The Outlook, said that a prominent Brazilian pointed out to him how the danger of color friction had been averted by Brazil's policy of race fusion, whereas in the United States color disagreements are more likely to increase. Second, and most important of all, the honor and dignity of the Republic demands a cessation of the dishonorable relations that have existed for more than three hundred years between white men and colored women."

"Amalgamation leads to degeneracy," persisted the senator with determination. "The mulatto is the inferior of both races. He inherits the bad qualities of both and the good traits of neither."

"No," objected No. 1, bending over to catch the eye of the senator, "that's impossible. How could it be possible for the mulatto to inherit the bad qualities of both races. He is inferior

FROM "SUPERMAN" TO MAN

only in longevity. I have seen aged white men and aged Negroes but never an aged mulatto. Why should the mulatto inherit the bad qualities of both races?"

A discussion between the two went on for some time. Dixon and the other passenger listened interestedly. "Here's where the doctors disagree," laughed Dixon to himself.

"They say the mulatto is the more vicious of the two races because he isn't so passive under exploitation as the full-blooded Negro," whispered passenger No. 2 to Dixon.

The latter took advantage of a short lull to refer them to the following quotation from Von Luschan, "We are absolutely ignorant about the moral and intellectual qualities of the half-castes," He added: "Roosevelt says: 'There is nothing of the mongrel about the aspect of the Brazilian.' Would you care to hear what Finot has to say on the subject?

Both assented. He found the place and began:—

"'Cross-breeding among the most differentiated races, far from resulting in sterility, adds to their fecundity. According to LeValliant, a Hottentot woman, who generally has three or four children, will have as many as ten or twelve when united to a white man or Negro. The crossing of Negroes with white women or white men with Negro women produces similar results.

"Cross-breeding has in no sense the sorry result of physical degeneracy nor of bringing peoples to final ruin. Where did Tylor find the most beautiful women in the world? At Tristan d'Acumha (a little island between the Cape and South America) among the descendants of whites and Negroes. . . . 'Among the young girls were some with such entirely beautiful heads, that I do not remember having seen anything so splendid. . . . And yet I am familiar with all the strands of the earth. Bali and its Malays, Havana and its Creoles, Tahiti and its nymphs, the United States and its most distinguished women.' "

Dixon closed the book and taking out his notebook said:—
"Dr. J. B. De Lacerda, director of the National Museum at Rio de Janeiro, Brazil, said in his address at the Universal Races Congress:

"'Galton's deductions in regard to hybridity in animals cannot be wholly applied to human half-breeds. In the case of man there is an inheritance of moral and intellectual qualities that follows no fixed and absolute rules. Under the influence of agencies of which we do not know the nature, the intellectual qualities often reach in the mixed progeny of the white and black a degree of superiority

FROM "SUPERMAN" TO MAN

which cannot be explained in terms of heredity either remote or proximate. Some unknown force gives rise in them to an intelligence that is capable of developing to a pitch neither of the parents could reach. It is, in fact, common to find as the offspring of a white of very mediocre intelligence united with a Negress of the lowest grade of culture an individual of considerable intellectual powers; just as if one of the effects of crossing in the case of man was precisely to improve the intelligence, or the moral and reflective qualities which distinguish individuals of the two races crossed.' "

He closed the notebook and added:—"Another important point to be noted is that our physiques conform to climatic environment. The Negro has been living in America for centuries. His constitution is therefore very likely to be similar to that of the native white, with the Negro possessing a better circulatory system and sounder tissue, due to greater physical exertion."

"But," objected No. 1, "the Negro is far more subject to tuberculosis of the lungs than the Caucasian."

"And the Indian, the only real American, is still more so than the Negro," replied Dixon. "According to the latest statistics I could find, that of the Bureau of American Ethnology for 1907-08, the Indian had 7.9 deaths per 1000 from this disease; the Negro had 4, and the Caucasian, 1.7. This disease is quite as common among the poorest classes of whites as among Negroes. According to the Chicago Herald, March 26, 1917, health commissioners found nearly three hundred cases in one white tenement block in that city. The white plague, like syphilis, is a white man's disease. He introduced both in the New World, but his superior wealth enables him better to combat them."

"You say syphilis is a white man's disease," said No. 1, "where did you get that?"

"So far as is known, it originated in Europe. Professor Elliott Smith examined ten thousand skeletons of ancient Egypt without finding any trace of it. Dr. Ales Hrdlicka of the Smithsonian Institute reports similarly of the pre-Columbian Indian. Syphilis like consumption cannot survive in primitive surroundings. At least, Livingstone, the great missionary to Africa, and a medical man, says, 'it dies out in the African interior' and that 'it seems incapable of permanence in any form in persons of pure African blood' in Africa. Syphilis first came into notice in the early part

FROM "SUPERMAN" TO MAN

of the sixteenth century when a great epidemic of it swept through Southern Europe. Assertion to the contrary has been examined by leading scholars and found to be false."

"But what about heredity that most important of all points to be considered in the crossing of animals, human or otherwise?" asked No. 1.

"A most important question, sir," replied Dixon, "and one that has been sadly neglected, as witness the welcome that was once extended to all types of European immigrants, nearly all of whom, except the German, French and Scandinavian, and possibly the English have always lived below the economic level of the American Negro. The Negro has a more intelligent and better-fed appearance than the average immigrant one saw at Ellis Island or in the steerage of trans-Atlantic liners. This is indisputable. The percentage of paupers among the foreign-born whites is almost five times that of the Negro. The figures, according to the census of 1910 are 284.2 and 63.9 per 100,000, respectively. Foreign-born whites as Italians, Syrians, Lithuanians, Poles, Albanians, all had a higher percentage of illiteracy than the Negro, according to the 1930 census. The Negro in New York State had one-third less illiteracy than the New York whites in 1930, and that was no doubt due to the large foreign white population.

"Anyway," said No. 1 with finality, "I still believe that every one should marry his own color. It doesn't look good to see a mixed couple."

"What would you think of the marriage of a full-blooded Negro to an octoroon, who was to all appearances white?" asked Dixon.

"That would be all right. They are both of the same race."

"And what would you think of the marriage of that same octoroon to another person, white, or believed to be white?"

"That would be wrong."

"But didn't you just say every one should marry his own color? In other words that black should marry white, brown browns, white whites, and blondes blondes?"

Passenger No. 2 who had hitherto been silent, now spoke.

"It is not a matter of whether it looks good," he said. "But whether it is right or wrong. Intermarriage, as the porter so

FROM "SUPERMAN" TO MAN

clearly showed us, is in accord with the law of Nature and of Nature's God. Physical affinity has ever been the principal motive in the mating of human beings, often regardless of racial differences. Ignore it as you will, the fact remains that there are a great many whites of both sexes who find their affinity, mental as well as physical, among Negroes; also many Negroes of both sexes, who find theirs among the whites. Most people in speaking about the inherent dislike the races have for each other forget that there is also an inherent attraction between them. From my observations and studies, which I flatter myself are pretty comprehensive, I see that Nature throughout all the ages and climes, simply refuses to submit to man-made laws and conventions, at least as far as the mixing of races is concerned. The vilifying of either of the races in question will not help since love is illogical. The harm done by laws against the marriage of blacks and whites is immense. Persons of the two so-called races, while often meeting clandestinely, get into the habit of shunning marriage even in those states where such a union is permissible. These restrictions also give many a convenient excuse for leading a double life, since while they may find their affinity in one of the other race they are conventionally bound to marry in their own. This artificial condition is, in short, responsible for a great amount of deception, especially on our part. Since so-called intermarriage does not mean the taking up of blacks and whites at random and marrying them off willy-nilly, but proceeds entirely from personal choice, I should think this matter revolves on the query.—'Should such persons be encouraged to live wedded or forced to live unwedded?' "

Dixon looked at this man with amazement, particularly as he knew him to be a Southerner. The senator had been keeping silent. He now challenged the speaker instantly. "You say you believe in miscegenation!" he said. "Tell me, would you have your daughter marry a nigger—a Negro."

"I'd never have any of my children married to anyone, white or black. I try to train them well. I teach them to discriminate between sincerity and insincerity, and leave them to choose their own partners. I should not exert any influence against anyone, of no matter what race. I think this is the only really civilized and democratic thing to do. And I'm not being

FROM "SUPERMAN" TO MAN

merely theoretical. My boy brings his Negro chum from college
to our house.

"With regard to amalgamation it strikes me that your talk
is at least two hundred years late. The fact is we have been
having amalgamation all along, let the ostriches deceive themselves as they will. Have you ever been to a Northern church,
a Northern school, or to a large gathering of Negroes? If so,
you will see so-called Negroes of every shade—from the purest
white to black—a sort of human race in miniature. I have
counted not less than thirty-four different shades. That's why
I had to smile when Benson said everyone should marry his
own color. Amalgamation has been taking place and although
under conditions that ought to be a disgrace to every self-respecting American good rather than evil has been the result. I went
to a large gathering of colored people recently and out of
thousands present, I saw less than a hundred that could be taken
as pure black. The audience appeared to be quite as healthy
and prosperous as the average white one—and certainly more
animated. I think that in view of the little or no restraint or
protest against illegal relations, and the strenuous objections to
legal ones, a cynic would be perfectly justified in saying that
the principal objection to so-called intermarriage is the legaliz-
ing of the union."

"One thing is sure," the senator said, "this racial intermixture
does not affect the racial integrity of the white man."

"Why?" said Dixon, much encouraged by his unexpected
ally.

"Because all mixed bloods are classed as Negroes. No blood
flows from the black race into the whites."

"Not all," retorted Dixon. "Intermixing of black and white
has been going steadily on for about three hundred years, so
much so that there is no stratum of American society in which
you will not find persons of mixed strain, and far more than
you think. I have heard it estimated at 60 per cent of the
native whites. The American Anglo-Saxon, composed of Slavs,
Latins, Jews, Teutons, Iranians, Celts, Indians, Magyars, Mon-
golians, and a comparatively small proportion of English, has
too, a considerable percentable of Negro strain. I have a colored
friend who is really more an Anglo-Saxon than many self-styled

FROM "SUPERMAN" TO MAN

Anglo-Saxons this side of the Atlantic—his paternal grandfather and his mother are English of old stock. Assertions of racial purity and integrity by any important people in the New World is not only absurd, but pathetic. Look at the very large number of presumably white persons with distinctly Negroid features! A little more pigment in their skins would make a radical change in their lives. Take New Orleans, for instance; the majority of the people there are no lighter than a Northern quadroon. A white Northerner who made his first trip to the South with me, on seeing the people of that city, said, "If you want to know who is white here, you'll have to get a blond!" How they distinguish for the jim-crow car simply puzzles me. In Texas where the whites are also mixed with Mexicans they are darker yet. You absolutely cannot tell the whites from some of the so-called Negroes. One of the whitest white persons I have ever met is a 'colored' woman. I would never have believed it if I hadn't seen her mother. Dr. Kintzung who made a careful study of the subject says it is impossible to tell persons with an attenuated strain of Negro blood, and Finot says that one can distinguish them only in American novels. Time and again persons that were thought to be white are proved to be of Negro descent. Henry Timrod, poet, perhaps the most outspoken advocate of the Confederacy, and to whom there is a statue in Charleston, S. C., was later discovered to be the son of a mulatto woman, named Hannah Caesar. Alexander Hamilton is generally believed to have been of Negro ancestry, though there is no actual proof of this. "Pure" white descent in the South, like paternity, must be conceded; it cannot be proved.

"And to no small extent in the North. You'll recall that it was possible in the 1920 election for the political enemies of President Harding to revive the old story that he was of Negro ancestry. Millions of Americans still believe that, and with cause, as it is possible to find any number of 'Negroes' who are even more Nordic in appearance than was Harding.

"As that gentleman there said a few minutes ago, amalgamation is actually taking place. It is taking place let the racial purists delude themselves as they will."

"You advocates of miscegenation!" said the senator, angrily, "always forget one important fact. You must shut your eyes

FROM "SUPERMAN" TO MAN

to the intense—the inherent—dislike between the two races.
You think——"

"Inherent dislike between the two races?" dominated Passenger No. 2. 'Do you believe in the Fatherhood of God? DO you?"

"Yes."

"Do you think then that the God who commanded us to love one another would create hate in the heart of one race for the other? Another question:—If this dislike is inherent why, why must it always be fed to keep it alive, like a furnace? This misunderstanding persists because it is so profitable to certain newspapers, politicians, Ku-Klux Klans and all the other exploiters of labor, white as well as black. Because also lustful white men want to keep Negro women at a stage where it will be easy to get them. Whatever dislike exists between the races today has been caused by training."

Dixon supported him: "The white man of his own volition has mixed with the black more than with any other variety of the human race and the exotic black is attracted rather than repelled by the white. In view of this fact it seems to me that one would be justified in saying that we have color attraction rather than color repulsion."

He took out his notebook and having found the desired passage, said, "Iwan Bloch, leading European sexologist, says in his book, 'The Sexual Life of Our Time,' page 614,—

" 'White men from very early times have had a peculiar weakness for Negresses and mulatto girls and women.

" 'The European newspapers are full of interesting reports of the powerful attractive force exercised by exotic individuals, male or female, such as Negroes, Arabs, Abyssinians, Moors, Indians, Japanese, etc., upon European men and women respectively. Whenever members of such races come to stay in any European capital, we hear of remarkable love affairs between the white girls and these strangers.

" 'The colored girl exercises a powerful attractive force upon the American man and even the proud American woman manifests with an especial frequency in Chicago a certain preference for the male Negro. But much greater is the alluring force exercised by the white upon the Negro."

FROM "SUPERMAN" TO MAN

"All of which shows how very artificial our segregation laws are," said passenger No. 2, at the same time asking Dixon the name of the book and noting it down. He continued: "I will tell you an incident that corroborates what you have just read: I happened to be in London at the time of Edward VII's coronation. To the event came many Africans, jet black and with the most superb physiques I have ever seen. The manner in which these men were petted and feted by women, even of the better class—many of whom had seen a black face for the first time—gave me food for much thought and reminded me strongly of that line in Shakespeare's 'Two Gentlemen of Verona': 'Black men are pearls in beauteous ladies' eyes!' I saw, too, where an American newspaper correspondent expressed her great disgust at the reception given to the Senegalese by the Parisiennes."

Neither of the two opponents responded.

Dixon continued: "Some time ago a Chicago newspaper in a crusade against cabarets advertised the fact that in certain ones owned by Negroes there was no color line and soon the majority of the patrons in those places were whites of both sexes. In one large Western city, where intermarriage is illegal, I found that the women who visited the colored clubs were all white. When I inquired as to the absence of colored women, I was told that the white men had appropriated them. The keeper of one of these places told me that several porters had lost their wives by bringing them to live in that city, and that he would not advise any colored man to bring his wife there. Ine one of these clubs I saw eight white women, five of whom were from the South. I also found in this city an ultra-private colored club where the better class of white women visited. I found similar relations existing between black and white in nearly all the large Western towns. In some of the latter the colored women who were few and usually of a very low class had nearly all gone over to the white man, being most scornful to colored men. "Who ordered any coal!" they would ask on the approach of a black man. All through the cities of the South I saw and heard of houses of prostitution whose occupants were black and patrons white, this being glaringly so in New Orleans. Similar conditions exist all over the United States and that part of Canada under American influence. In one large Eastern city,

FROM "SUPERMAN" TO MAN

I found a club, run by a white man for railroad porters, where all the women in it were white. In Chicago there are scores of resorts where Negroes meet white women and white men black women. The sexual relations between black and white whether they exist in Boston, San Francisco, Seattle, or New Orleans, are of chronic immorality."

No protest from the opposing side.

Dixon continued: "But if there be an inherent dislike between these two groups of our citizens why make anti-miscegenation laws? If there be a great gulf fixed, why make segregation laws? Isn't restraint the purpose of law? Anti-marriage laws give the whole thing away. They furnish strong circumstantial evidence that whites do want to mate with blacks. A law prohibiting marriage on account of color is unnatural, immoral and stupid, and a monument to the asininity of those who make it. Hostile to one of the most elementary laws of Nature, it will not prevail. In states where such a law is in force I have noticed only a greater immorality. In the South white men have marked certain colored women as their own and the Negro who attempts to take them away does so at the risk of his life. It is no uncommon thing for white men to kill Negroes because of this. This is axiomatic: Forbid a human being anything whatsoever and you at once excite in him a desire to possess it. Tobacco won its way to popularity among white people because of the severe law against it. A follower of Mahomet was once asked that prophet's reason for forbidding the use of wine to his adherents. He replied, 'So that they might find the greater zest in its enjoyment.' Stolen waters, says the proverb, are the sweetest. In the past even the leading aristocrats have not hesitated to mingle their blood with the Negro, and they are still doing it in spite of all laws and conventions. The mixing of races is a law of nature just like gravitation or radio-activity It has always existed It is rolling along with the momentum of aeons and mortal man is powerless to stop it."

"As proved by three hundred years of anti-miscegenation laws," supported No. 2.

"But," said No. 1. "The black man is always more willing to marry the white woman than the white man to marry the

FROM "SUPERMAN" TO MAN

black woman!"

"That brings us to the real reasons for these laws: the prevention of the Negro man from participating in the mixing," said Dixon. "It's the same old case of 'what's mine, 's mine, and what's yours is mine and yours,' crystallized and made to function as law. As long as the white woman is left out miscegenation is considered perfectly proper. A good many Southern whites, perhaps the majority, consider the comely Negro lass their legitimate prey. Under these laws Negro women have absolutely no protection, as in the case of a sixteen year old girl who was wronged by a Los Angeles policeman, and who under the California anti-marriage law had no redress. But in view of the great amount of mixing done and being done by the whites and the small number of marriages contracted by them, doesn't it appear a greater honor and morality on the part of the Negro that he should desire to marry and have his children born in wedlock?"

"That's true, conceded No. 1, "I must admit that the white man even while legislating against miscegenation has always practised it." With a sly wink at the senator, he added: "Each feels that the law applies only to the other fellow, and gosh! how sore it makes him to see it broken."

"What's more," said No. 2, "the Caucasian has never been among any people, however degraded, that he did not mix with them—Hottentots, Bushmen, Fijians, Dyaks, Igorrotes, Maoris, —all. A mixture of white blood is the easiest of all to get. And what is easy to get is never worth very much; is it?"

"But it is only white women of the abandoned class—prostitutes and others who marry Negroes," said the senator.

"That is the current belief," replied Dixon, "but it is wrong in the vast majority of cases. In Chicago there are hundreds of mixed couples. These couples have no less than four fraternities—Manasseh societies, as they are called. I have been to their balls and parties and visited a good deal in their homes. These women are not a whit different from the ordinary respectable American woman, white or black. Most of them have fine well-kept homes, well-regulated families and live as happily as the problem imposed on them will grant."

FROM "SUPERMAN" TO MAN

"And with reference to the abandoned white women who do marry Negroes: may not their reason for doing so be that they find in the black man that which their own people had refused them—that lack in their lives which had made outcasts of them—genuine human sympathy?"

"Another point," persisted the senator, "If either parent has a drop of Negro blood, be it ever so small, the child is liable to be born coal black with thick lips and kinky hair."

"The Carnegie Institute," said Dixon, "had two of its expert pedigree tracers to dig in this matter for a whole year and they could not find a single substantiated case. This canard of the apparently unmixed white couple with the coal-black baby is like ghosts. Most everyone believes in them, but no entirely sane person has ever seen one.

"One of the pedigree tracers was Dr. C. B. Davenport, distinguished eugenist, who has studied the mixed-bloods in America, the West Indies, and Australia. He said that a child is hardly ever likely to be darker in color than the darker of the two parents.

"Once in Cardiff, Wales, I saw a white woman with a baby so very dark that I doubted it was really hers till I saw her husband, who was a native African of purest type. However, the child was less dark than the father.

"If no white women ever went with Negroes, I could accept that story of a white couple with a Negro child as due to atavism. But you'll find any number of white women, married and otherwise, having mulatto children as the result of intercourse with Negroes. Why, then, go to the moon for an explanation of the white couple with a black baby when a logical reason lies right under our nose?

"But if the child were born black, what of it!" asked No. 1, hasn't it a human soul?"

He added: "In view of these two facts:—first, that intermarriage is contrary neither to the laws of God nor of Nature; second, that persons who have a desire for one another's society are going to meet in spite of all laws, it is clear, unless we admit our ignorance, that the sole purpose and effect of anti-marriage laws are, the upholding of racial vanity, even to the detriment of morality and good citizenship."

THIRD DAY

"Oh, give me liberty,
For were a paradise itself my prison
Still I should long to leap the crystal walls."
—Dryden.

The next day at noon Dixon was sitting in an end seat contemplating the snow-covered wastes when Passenger No. 2 approached him and sitting in the opposite seat said: "Did I understand you to say you have been in South America?" And the passenger, who had also travelled in South America, engaged him in a conversation about Argentina. The talk gradually led to conditions among the Negroes in the South. Among other things the passenger said, was: "I am a Southerner myself, but I am very much opposed to the South's treatment of the Negro. The South, generally speaking, badly needs an infusion of new ideas. At present it is like an ancestral mansion, whose occupants, sitting behind shuttered windows that barely admit the sunlight, are still basking in the reflection of the dubious glory of the past. The South's pride of race is tragic. Pride of race made Spain what it was—a nation of decayed aristocrats and illiterate superstitious peasants. How I wish my beloved Southland would throw open the windows of its soul and let in the rejuvenating sunlight of truth.

"And the South can never rise higher than the Negro. Black and white in the South are like Siamese Twins who, while they are physiologically distinct beings, are so joined that one of the twins could not harm the other without harming himself, or benefit the other without benefiting himself."

Dixon took occasion to compliment him on his broadmindedness.

"Well," he went on to say, "I've found truth the only thing worth living for. But there is a hard struggle to obtain it. As a rule, we do not like to hear that which doesn't fit with our own ideas. I find that when it comes to unpleasant truths my mind shies like a horse at strange objects. By constant use of the spur, Reason, however, I force my will to accustom itself to strange truths—to overcome prejudice—and so I go on finding each new truth easier to accept."

FROM "SUPERMAN" TO MAN

"Many of our most prominent men, leaders of thought, are conspicuously weak-kneed on this matter of color," he continued. "They dread public opinion. By a good many people I am regarded as a freak or an open enemy. Some even say that I must be a Negro. But I would rather be anything else than a coward or one of those who take opinions from leaders who are out to serve themselves."

"Leaders! There lies the difficulty," said Dixon. "The masses pick their leaders according to their, the masses', own light. Each one picks the way in which he finds the greatest pleasure in giving up his money."

"That's it. It takes money to do anything these days, I know; but if Christ is the typical leader of men how few approach him. There is no record of Christ ever taking up a collection. Leaders, however, are a necessity and they must be supported if they are to work at all. I make it a point never to give a cent to any leader who appeals to me on any ground other than justice for all, regardless of color, creed or class. No segregations. Every American citizen must be free to go anywhere and to do anything that any other law-abiding citizen is free to do. That's my stand. I say with DeFoe:

"'He that hath truth on his side is a fool as well as a coward if he is afraid to own it because of the currency or multitude of men's opinion.'"

"I owe a great deal to my Negro mammy," he continued. "I shall never forget her tender care for my mother and me during the hard time after the war, and her forgiving Christian character. More than any other agency, that of my parents not excepted, she has been a power for molding me for good. My people say that the Negro is a hindrance to their progress. Yes, he is, but because of themselves. In other words, he is the prisoner; they are the jailers. No jailer is ever a free man, himself. Thoughts of the Negro, and how to keep him a common laborer predominate in the Southern mind today. Since whatever dwells uppermost in our mind rules us, the South actually has what it dreads most—Negro domination. And ah,—how different things could be!"

FROM "SUPERMAN" TO MAN

Both men exchanged views until the announcement of luncheon. Before leaving for the dining car the passenger said: "The United States, in its treatment of the Negro would do well to imitate the humble oyster, who, when a grit or a worm or whatever it be, gets into his shell, quietly makes the irritant into a pearl. And believe me!" he continued in a voice so kindly, so full of his creed of right doing that it affected Dixon's innermost being and pervaded him with its sincerity, "no other race that I know of possesses the qualities for conversion into human pearls as the Negro—kindly, sunny, faithful!"

That night, while Dixon was cleaning the cuspidors, the senator came in with a newspaper. After reading for a few minutes, he inquired:—"Dixon, I have been wondering why a man of your intelligence should stay in a job like this!" He knew the reason well, but he wanted to hear what the other had to say.

Dixon suspended the cleaning to tell him what he had told the Frenchman. He added: 'I recently passed an examination for a secretaryship in the United States Consular service. But," he laughed, "as I had to submit a picture of myself I shall be very much surprised if I get an appointment."

"Have you ever thought of leaving the United States to live abroad?"

"Yes, I have thought of going to Brazil, but on second thoughts, I have decided to remain here. Sometimes I feel as if I am experiencing too much of the acid of color prejudice to keep my temper sweet. But," he added with determination, "this is my country, mine as much as any other American's. My great-great-grandfather died to win the freedom of this country at the battle of Rhode Island, August 29, 1778; my great-grandfather fought to preserve its independence at Lake Erie in 1812; my grandfather fought at Shiloh to preserve its unity, and I myself have seen a little active service. I am an American—a plain American —and one I shall remain in spite of all the attempts to hyphenate me. I am going to fight it out here even as my forefathers did. No one shall make me run."

"Yet, there are many Negroes who hold federal jobs in Washington."

FROM "SUPERMAN" TO MAN

"Yes, some hold fairly good positions," replied Dixon, "but since prejudice is an enemy that will not permit open competition, it is often a matter of the merest chance that they get these often well-merited positions. Color egotism, thus diverting valuable talent into lines of employment that could be filled by persons more fitted for them, is bad economics. A vast amount of Negro talent and genius goes to absolute waste. This woefully short-sighted policy results in a direct loss to the nation."

"But so many Negroes are without any ambition at all," said the senator. "You said that there are better opportunities in the North, but in all the large Northern cities it seems to me that the proportion of Negroes hanging outside saloons and loafing in pool-rooms was far in excess of those white doing the same thing."

"Perhaps so," replied Dixon, "but consider the bad example these have. The educated and ambitious Negro is often forced into competition with his uneducated brother, who, seeing the former faring no better than he, often bossed by one whose chief asset is his complexion, has no incentive to step out. But today at dinner I heard one of the porters say: 'What's the use? There's Dixon with a good education and he is doing the same porter work as I." There I was actually setting a bad example to this man! Now, really, can you blame them for this Omar Khayyam outlook? What incentive have they? It might be said that these men had little or no ambition to start with. Perhaps so. But the duty we owe to our fellow-men, is not to throw obstacles in their way, but to encourage them, to fan every spark of ambition. The aspiring Negro is severely handicapped in his desire to accomplish anything. He has to wrestle so long and so hard with prejudice that a great portion of his energy is lost. Take the case of a poor Negro at a university. While the poor white student can get any spare time position, the Negro has to depend on the color whims of the employer. Even the meanest jobs are sometimes refused him. As a student I was once refused a job of taking out soiled dishes in return for my meals on account of color. It is truly disheartening to see Negro youths being graduated, after the severest struggles, to find the door of opportunity closed in their faces. As an instance, take Chicago. Nation-wide experience tells me that the Negro

FROM "SUPERMAN" TO MAN

has better opportunities there than anywhere else. Yet the disadvantages of colored people suffer in that city, as reported by the Juvenile Protective Association, are unbelievable. I happen to have a clipping from the report in my grip and would like to show it to you."

He left the room returning soon with the clipping, which he handed to the senator. The latter glanced at it a moment and handed it back saying: "Would you mind reading it for me?"

Dixon read:

" 'In the business world—speaking generally—the discrimination against the Negro is even greater. It grows more and more difficult for a colored man or woman to get work except as a laborer or servant and even in those directions there are serious difficulties. As salespeople, office clerks, and stenographers, there is almost no opportunity for Negroes in Chicago. With one exception the big business colleges discriminate against colored students. There is small encouragement for them to take training in technical courses in public schools. One bright colored boy who graduated from a technical school this year was sent with his classmates to the employment office of a big corporation. 'We don't hire niggers,' said the main in charge.' "

Dixon added, "A conspicuous example of an employer who does the reverse of the above is Henry Ford. In his Detroit plant Negroes work at anything for which they are fit—inventors, designers, machinists, office-work. Ford is a genuine American."

A child's cry was heard in the body of the car. Dixon asked to be excused and hurried in. A few minutes later he returned bringing a baby about eighteen months old.

"His mama has train sickness," explained Dixon.

The youngster, riding on Dixon's knee and tickled by the senator was now laughing and kicking with delight. Dixon, by tossing him and riding him around for the past two days had been spoiling him. Several times he had refused to return to his mother.

The child soon became sleepy again, and nestling in Dixon's arms, was soon sound asleep.

He resumed the reading of the clipping.

" 'Out of nearly 4,000 men employed by the express companies, only twenty-one are colored men, and fifteen of that number work as porters. There are apparently none at all employed as boot and shoe hands, glovemakers, bindery workers, printers, neck-wear and suspender workers or on the elevated roads. A good many labor unions admit colored men to membership, but these complain that they are discriminated against, at least in the more difficult and better-paid trades, when it comes to getting work.

" 'The result is that the mass of Negroes are forced to seek, in increasing numbers, the less desirable and poorly-paid occupations. More Negro men—nearly 8,000 in all—work as porters and bar helpers in saloons and poolrooms than in any other field.' "

"This report," explained Dixon, "depicts conditions of some years ago, but they are substantially true of all Northern cities now."

"What do you think of the education of the Negro," next asked the senator.

Dixon thought the question vague, but answered, "I do not think it ought to differ from that of any other color of mankind. Every human being regardless of sex, ought to be permitted to develop his or her fullest powers, in his or her own way. Any agency that prevents this is pernicious in the extreme. Is it to the benefit of the state that certain of its citizens be forcibly dwarfed to remain laborers? In the reign of Henry VIII, the lower classes were not permitted to read the Bible, particularly the New Testament. How do we of today view that? Yet, here five hundred years later we find men in authority advocating an analogous thing in non-education of certain citizens."

"But the ignorant Negro is the happy Negro,"—protested the senator. "To educate him is only to make him unhappy."

"Very well," replied Dixon, "here is this sleeping infant. He is ignorant and hence is always happy when healthy, and well-cared for. Would you always keep him at this stage because education and the knowledge of life will make him unhappier as it surely will?"

"Again, with the possible exception of the Latin races, the Caucasian is the unhappiest of all peoples. Now, suppose I were to say, 'Do not educate white men any more; to do so is only to make them unhappier,' what would you think of me? Advocates of non-education for Negroes have shown so little regard for us in other vital matters and so much genuine solicitude in this that I have begun to suspect that what they

FROM "SUPERMAN" TO MAN

really mean is: Do not educate the Negro and make the unhappy white man, unhappier."

The senator did not reply. Dixon continued: "Moreover, the thinker of any color is often unhappy because education enables him to see the tinsel and the heartaches; the injustices and the greed that go to make up the greater part of our civilization. But, as you say, there is some mercy in this advocacy of non-education of the Negro for while the uneducated Negro of the United States has a far happier lot than any other peasant class perhaps in the world, there is no recognized place in America for the educated Negro. To use an old phrase: he is in advance of his age, that is, so far as conditions are governed by the whites. He lacks that association that helped to make Johnson, Lamb, Coleridge, and Garrick what they were. Solomon said: 'He that increaseth knowledge increaseth sorrow.' This statement is especially true of educated Negroes. The ignorant Negro like the ignorant white man will continue to be the happier one until we educate or remove the cause that makes the thinking ones of both races unhappy, namely, the greedy white men and the few greedy Negroes at the top."

"A great many advocate only industrial training for the Negro," said the senator. "What do you think of that? I favor industrial training; since that is the basis of all production, the race will acquire wealth and independence. If the Negro cannot get employment among white people, he must create work for himself. The great trouble with the Negro race is, that it has too many doctors, lawyers and preachers."

"When you say that the Negro should start out for himself," replied Dixon, "it is equivalent to saying that here amidst this wealth of development, distilled by the human race from the bitter experiences of thousands of years, certain human beings should start in again like troglodytes. In these days of express trains should one be compelled to travel in a prairie schooner until he has learnt to build his own railway? Why impose on us conditions that you'd be the first to kick against if applied to you? It should be just as logical to ask, 'What form of training is preferable for white men?' As no two men are alike human intellect cannot be regimented. Any such attempt, besides preventing full attainment, will cause unhappiness. Everyone,

FROM "SUPERMAN" TO MAN

as Shakespeare advises, should study what he most affects. I say let everyone, white as well as black, be permitted to pick out his own occupation and follow it without interference. In this way and this way only will the great curse of civilization,—uncongenial employment,—be removed.

"You also spoke of the large number of Negro doctors, lawyers and preachers, and the relatively small number in the mechanical pursuits. I happen to have the figures here. The census of 1930 shows: One white doctor for every 726 whites; one Negro doctor for every 3099 Negroes; lawyers, white, one in 686; Negroes, one in 9536; preachers, one for every 869 whites; one for every 471 Negroes."

"Well, I was right about the preachers, anyway."

"According to the white ratio you are. It gives us almost two to one. You see, the Negroes having few of the sweets of this life, have strong hope of getting theirs after they have been put under the sod. The white man's religion promises this very strongly to them, and also to those whites who are similarly deprived. Since the Negro's forte is religion, he is more easily exploited in that field, and since to become a preacher in any group, regardless of race, the chief essential is the gift of gab, the sharpers, who among the whites would be lawyers and speculators, among Negroes simply gravitate to the ministry and also to hair and complexion doctoring."

The train began to slow down as the lights of a town were visible nearby.

"What place is this?" asked the senator.

"Evanston, Wyo."

"How long do we stay?"

"About five minutes. We change engines."

"I think I'll take a walk then."

Dixon took the sleeping child to his mother and went to the drawing-room for the senator's hat and overcoat. Later both left the smoker and went out on the vestibule. As Dixon opened the trap-door a rush of icy air swept in, compelling the senator to button up his overcoat around his neck.

"Pretty cold!" he said, hopping around.

"It gets a bit cold up here on the mountains. It's about 25 below tonight."

FROM "SUPERMAN" TO MAN

The train stopped and both stepped off into the crisp midnight air. The senator saw the sign of the railroad lunchroom.

Have we time for a cup of coffee?" he asked hurriedly.

"Yes, sir."

"Come along, then," he said, catching Dixon by the coatsleeve. Dixon left the car in charge of the sleeping-car conductor and both men started on a trot over the crackling snow for the lunch-room.

The senator ordered coffee and sandwiches for Dixon and himself. After a few mouthfuls the senator began to look nervously through the window.

"We've plenty of time, sir," reassured Dixon, guessing the cause of his anxiety. "See! there's the train-conductor just getting his lunch now!"

When the train started again the senator, followed by Dixon, returned to the smoker. Throwing his hat and overcoat on the seat, the senator settled himself comfortably in the chair.

"Let me see," he said after a few contemplative puffs of his cigar, "we were last speaking of Negro education, weren't we? I—I—" he continued haltingly, as a thought struck him like a dart—he had just become conscious of the fact that he had just dined with a Negro! Dixon had been conscious of the incident all along. When the senator recovered his composure he said:

"What do you think of the late leader of your race, Booker T. Washington? I should judge that you are against his policies."

"If it is his policy of advocating the surrender of certain rights for progress in other directions that you mean, sir, I am, on conditions. Booker T. Washington has been much blamed, and is still being blamed, for not standing up more firmly for the rights of his people. A book-agent told me that he had difficulty in selling Washington's book among colored people. Many would-be patrons, he said, refused, saying that they did not like the way in which he had bowed to the white man. But even had Booker T. been endowed with an unbending spirit I cannot see how he could have done otherwise and have carried out his life work. The great majority of the people that needed his help were in the South, where any assertion of Negro rights,

FROM "SUPERMAN" TO MAN

would, as you know, not only have been resented, but might have
been accompanied with serious results. Had he shown a defiant
spirit, there would simply have been no Tuskegee, and schools
with the spirit of Tuskegee were, and still are, a necessity for
both white and colored. The majority of any race is fit only
for industrial pursuits; this would be particularly true of a people
but recently freed. And humble as was his manner, there were
those whites who complained that Tuskegee, with its thorough-
ness, was making not servants, but masters, thus threatening white
domination. Booker T. Washington has done more than any
other person or agency that I know of toward guiding the feet
of the crude, struggling mass of freedmen to the first rung of the
ladder of progress. It is true that others will have to strive hard
to undo the impression he gave of Negro subordination yet the
blame for this should be placed on the conditions to which he
was forced to adapt himself in order to do his work. But whatever one may say of his methods no one can impugn the honesty
of his motives. This was a genuine desire born of the largeness
of his heart to do good. Booker T. Washington built his fame
on the surest of all foundations—unselfish service. Some object
that he made a great deal of money. I sincerely hope he did, for
I know of no other American who deserved it better than he.
There are a very few of his critics, black or white, indeed, few
citizens of any country who would not do well to emulate his
unselfishness, his energy, and his persistence.

"And yet, some rightly resented the title that was given him,
leader of the Negro race. He did not have the spirit of a leader,
that is, if Hampden, Toussaint L'Overture, George Washington,
Frederick Douglass, Pinckney, or Patrick Henry had that spirit.
The spirit of surrender so much admired in Booker Washington by many whites is just the opposite of what these same
whites would like to see in their people under similar conditions—is just what they have always condemned most. We hear
a great deal of praise for the slave who stayed at home guarding
his master's property while the master was gone off to war to
tighten his chains. Very well, what is your opinion of the white
men who advised surrender to King George, and remained loyal
to him during the Revolutionary War? I think that if those
slaves had had a spark of self-respect left in them they would

FROM "SUPERMAN" TO MAN

have taken everything of value they could have set their hands on and escaped killing, if possible, anyone hindering their flight. The mission of republics is to foster and stimulate self-respect in mankind—to let every man and every woman feel that he or she is an indispensable entity in the universe. There ought to be no cringing or kowtowing to caste of any kind.

"Of course this policy of eating humble pie is the best one by which Negroes can get money. But is money everything? Can it buy self-respect? I think that one spark of that kingliness of soul which, while respecting superior merit, recognizes no artificial nobility, whether of caste or color, gives more genuine satisfaction in the long run than all the wealth of a Rockefeller. If the black man ever hopes to gain the respect of the whites he will have to make a determined stand for his rights, regardless of the cost."

"But," said the Senator, "the Negro is poor, and a poor man cannot afford to talk strongly."

"He is poor," replied Dixon, "but whose fault is it? In 1865, after 250 years of unpaid toil, if he had received justice, nothing less than the transference of the entire South into his hands would have been the result. But no one who has the spirit of real manhood is ever poor. With that as a foundation all things are possible. 'My mind to me a kingdom is,' said a poet."

The senator did not reply.

Dixon continued: "A matter of pigment can furnish no excuse for two so diametrically opposed policies in this nation. What is right for one body of citizens must be right for other citizens, living among them and subject to the same laws. Segregation of any kind is injustice. Why set a man aside if you do not wish to treat him differently? 'There can no more be two kinds of right,' says Huxley, 'than there can be two kinds of straight lines.' Moreover, this policy of flattery is bad for white men or any other sort of men. If the Negro really wishes to even up scores with the white man,—I speak of the South—he should keep on flattering him and thus at one coup undermine both his character and his purse."

The bell called Dixon away. When he returned ten minutes later the senator was reading a newspaper he had bought in the lunch-room. He called Dixon's attention to an account of a

FROM "SUPERMAN" TO MAN

lynching and asked him what he thought about it.

Taking the paper Dixon read:—

"NEGRO BURNED BY MOB OF CHEERING TEXANS. THOUSANDS, INCLUDING YOUNG GIRLS, SEE BLACK BURNED ALIVE AT STAKE IN PUBLIC SQUARE."

"That such a thing should be possible in a country which more than any other on earth proclaims its civilization!" said Dixon. "Can the most savage South Sea tribe equal in barbarity the infamous lynching record of this republic with tis vast number of churches, colleges, and schools? When before in the history of the human race, from its darkest moment until now, has there been another country where a citizen could be dismembered, burnt alive, and every other form of atrocity, which fiendish ingenuity can devise be inflicted upon hin simply because he refuses to get off a sidewalk or gives a saucy word to another? Even the shocking crime of rape, which is falsely alleged as being the incentive for these outbursts of ferocity, offers not the slightest excuse. Rape is as old as the human race. It exists in all climes and among every race on earth. If white men were being burned alive for this crime how many, think you, would be burned in America daily? We have had so much lynching, and with so much acquiescence that it has become a recognized American institution. Indeed, from what I have just read it is one of our outdoor sports. The conscience of the nation is numb, that is, if it ever had any conscience at all. How we shudder at the barbarity of the pagan who two thousand years ago, used to burn Christians alive! Yet we let pass almost unnoticed the burning of Christians by Christians today in our own midst. The Roman pagan used to have a holiday and flock from afar to see Christians tortured. Today the Christians of Georgia, Texas, Illinois and Minnesota are doing or have done the same thing. Let it be a vicious mule that was burnt alive; how those tender-hearted Christian sadists would howl. And the better element acquiesces in these atrocities for the murderers are rarely, if ever brought to justice. Even with pictures, taken by the murderers themselves and circulated far and wide, the officers of the so-called law find it impossible to identify a single lyncher and the jury returns the stereotyped verdict, death by parties unknown.'

FROM "SUPERMAN" TO MAN

"The direct cause of lynching is the catering of the presumed better classes to the ignoble spirit in the lower classes here in America. Why do the supposed better classes cater to the lower classes? Why don't our legislators stop it? Why don't our presidents with the power of the army and the navy behind them? Is it because they don't know it is wrong? Well, kill a song-bird or catch a fish out of season, in short, do anything they don't want you to do, and see if they wouldn't stop you, if they had to call out the entire army and navy!

"No, lynching isn't stopped, not because it can't be, but because the majority of our law-makers and rulers for the past fifty years have been and are a part of that system of exploitation that would suffer were lynching stopped. The lyncher is but the tool of his system. Every man, be he scavenger or president, who upholds this theory of color inferiority is an aider and abettor of lynching in the same manner that every rivulet and raindrop helps to swell the river. Lynching is but the culmination of this doctrine of the superiority of unpigmented skin and flossy hair.

"But national acquiescence in lynching does not minimize the horror of it to the really cultured. Think of the excruciating pain of even a burnt finger, then imagine the whole body in flames! The upholders of chivalry in olden times would strive singly against a host of foes. Hereward, Roland, and DuGues-clin were happiest when attacking many foes at the same time but the chevaliers of the South, who brag of these great men as if they were their immediate fathers, hunt in packs like wolves. Thousands of these gallants will attack a single Negro, whom more likely than not, they would run from singly. Southern chivalry is as brutal, dastardly and debasing as olden chivalry was reputed brave, magnanimous and ennobling. Having roasted their victim, these upholders of Southern womanhood will rend the reeking flesh in search of trophies, bequeathing them as a rich legacy unto their issue. I once saw a Southern gentleman exhibiting with great pride a member torn from a lynched Negro. 'Could the lynchers of Georgia be any worse if they had belonged to any other than the Christian religion?' asked Ingersoll. I ask—'Could they be more barbarous if they belonged to any other than the white race?" I see no differ-

FROM "SUPERMAN" TO MAN

ence whatever between the spirit prompting white Americans to cut off the fingers and toes of black men and women and that which used to incite the Fiji Islander to cut off the fingers and toes of white men before civilization came to him.

"And very often these victims are absolutely innocent. Of the tens of thousands of Negroes lynched in riots and massacres in the past forty years the vast majority committed no crime whatever. The mob is usually never satisfied with one victim. Like the Australian Bushman of the old days or the barbarous Jews in the days of Joshua who would attack even the family of an offender, American whites usually hold all Negroes to blame for the fault of one. Just so long as lynching continues we will be hypocrites when we point to the barbarity of any other country, Mexico, for example, which abolished race distinction as early as 1824, and thus is a far more civilized place than the Southern States. Really, these best citizens, these would-be Chesterfields are nothing else than common murderers, cowardly to the core. These sadists would be tolerated in no other country.

"Lynching will not be stopped until we acquire some national pride—I mean real national self-respect like the Englishman or Frenchman has. And God only knows when we will! After a hundred and fifty years of self-government, perhaps the only tangible evidence of this is that optimistic drivel about the land of the free and the home of the brave."

The senator did not reply. Dixon looked out of the window and remarked:—"We're now in Utah."

"The Mormon State, eh? Tell me, have the Mormons at present more than one wife?"

"I have been credibly informed that polygamy still persists, and that some of the older Mormoms have as many as four wives, secretly, of course."

"Four wives; Well—that mightn't be so bad, but four mothers-in-law! Holy catamounts!"

After conversing for some time in this vein, the senator returned to the original conversation. "What were you saying about Mexico and racial distinctions?" he asked.

"When I spoke I had in mind this particular case. Between El Paso, Texas, and Juarez, Old Mexico, there is a street railway

FROM "SUPERMAN" TO MAN

Negroes, on the American side, are compelled to ride jim-crow. As soon as they reach the Mexican side, however, they may move to any part of the car they wish. Now if the equality of treatment of its citizens is the test of the degree of civilization of any country, and it certainly is, is not Mexico more civilized than the Southern states and the United States in general. The whole system of racial distinction in America is a farce. For instance, a citizen who would be white in Indiana or Oregon would be Negro in Kentucky, according to the jim-crow law of those states. Some states say that one-eighth or more Negro blood makes a Negro, others one-sixteenth, one-thirty-second and so on. The question is: Just when is an American citizen black and when is he white?

"How can one with the least reasoning ability call this mixture of almost every human variety under the sun, Negro. What would our brilliant American anthropologists call, for instance, a man who is half-Indian and half-Mongolian. If a Kruman is a Negro, how can a man who is fifteen parts white, and one part Kruman, still be a Negro? Why is a man who is three parts an Indian, and one part white, still an Indian?

"But I do not intend to cavil at names. The terms, Caucasian, Aryan, White Man, are all misnomers. And why aren't the whites so hot and bothered about names as the Negroes? Because the whites are on top. Women, too, don't like being called females, but what man ever gives it a second thought when called a male?

"Far too much energy is spent by brainless Negroes who believe that a change to some other name would make them appear better in white eyes. But for a man that's in prison what does it matter to those who are keeping him there whether he calls himself convict, prisoner, or inmate. His first thought should be how to be free. Some Negroes insist on colored, but is not the jim-crow car, the greatest insult to them and to American citizenship, marked 'Colored?' Yes, far too many Negroes mistake an inferiority complex for race pride.

"The value of names rises and falls just like the value of a bank-book. The term Anglo-Saxon was once a term of reproach and so was Christian, Quaker and Samaritan. It is not the name but the man himself that counts. If the term, Negro, persists

FROM "SUPERMAN" TO MAN

it will become an honorable one."

"Indeed;" sniffed the senator.

"Yes, the Negro has been having a vital task to perform here in America. . . ."

"Such as what?"

"Such as re-infusing into the national stock that vigor necessary for its perpetuation. Eugenists and sociologists say that since 1876 there had been a marked vitiation of European stock in all the countries of Europe, except Russia. The war has quickened the process of decay in all Europe. This nation has been fed from the European stream of immigration. It is the foreign element that has kept America going; therefore with a decayed supply the result is evident. In my belief, what the Caucasian needs as a rejuvenator particularly in the South—where the vitiation of the Caucasian stock is glaringly apparent—is an infusion of blood from some primitive stock, with nerves and tissues unspoiled by the greed of civilization, like the magnificent Zulu; that is, if this primitive stock would stand for it, which I very much doubt. The Negro with his fresher, more buoyant mentality can do a great deal toward relieving the tension on the nerves of the Caucasian. For instance, the statistics of 1913 show one suicide for every 8,500 whites; one for every 36,000 colored; white insane, one in 469; Negro, one in 761; whites are also more prone to the use of drugs and to sadistic acts, such as lynching and mob-violence—all signs of bad nerves. President Rittenhouse of the Life Extension Institute gave twenty causes for the decreasing vitality of the people of this nation and the chief was nervous strain. I think it is for this reason then—repairing the ravages made by civilization, that Nature has with its usual prevision, deposited this balance from its reserve fund—the Negro—here in America."

Dixon found a passage in his notebook and said: "Sir Harry Johnston in his address before the Universal Races Congress said:

"'He (the Negro) has certainly been endowed by Nature with a degree of race fertility probably far surpassing that of the European, Asiatic, and American Indian living under conditions similarly unfavorable to the struggle for existence. Those few scientific men in Britain, Germany, France, the United States and Brazil, who have

FROM "SUPERMAN" TO MAN

striven to understand the anthropology of the Negro and to compare it with the white man are rather inclined than otherwise to argue now that the Negro and the Negroids have contributed in the past, and still more may contribute in the future, a very important quota to the whole sum of humanity—an element of soundness and stability in physical development and certain mental qualities which the perfected man of, let us say twenty or twenty-two centuries after Christ, cannot afford to do without.' "

Dixon added, "In the 1917 to 1918 drafts, the Negro according to Provost-Marshal's report, proved 5 per cent more physically fit than the white man. The figures are: Negro, 74.60; white, 69.71."

The senator appeared to be thinking deeply. After a few moments he asked:—"How do you account for the higher criminality of the Negro? He is nearly four times as criminal as the white man."

"It is due, first of all to the injustice he receives from the officers of the law. Justice, when a Negro is brought before her, particularly in the Southern States, discards her scales and takes a firmer grip on her sword. Most of the offenses of Negroes are against property, or are caused by low wages. Negroes are poorer than whites and you will find more of them in prison for the same reason that you will find more poor whites in prison than rich ones. Again, Negroes are more illiterate—some are in entire ignorance of certain laws. The whites make little or no effort to get education to them, sometimes actually prevent it, and yet expect those poor ignorant people to know, and to be acquainted with the complexities of civilization. People often break laws for the same reason that strangers to foreign countries commit breaches of custom. Further, in most of the Southern states it is a case of 'the king can do no wrong.' White men may wrong Negroes with impunity, while the Negro who offends a white person is severely punished. You probably recall the case of the arch-murderer Williams on the Georgia Death Farm. For the proven murder of eleven Negroes it was only after a severe battle and the world-wide publicity given the crime that Williams received life-imprisonment. But had it been a case of a Negro even wounding a white person! Were all the whites who are wronging Negroes punished, it is not too much to say that in states like Mississippi, jail life would be the normal life.

FROM "SUPERMAN" TO MAN

"Another cause for the large number of Negroes in prison is that in states like Georgia and Florida where peonage prevails, whenever the politicians need money all that they have to do is to arrest Negroes for some trivial or fancied cause, have them sentenced to a year or so, and sell them to some employer and pocket the proceeds. In short, the whites are directly responsible for a very large percentage of Negro criminality. Finot rightly asks, 'After all, can one ask of a race exasperated by all kinds of barbarous and unjust treatment that self-respect and moral dignity which constitute the best barriers against criminal leanings?' It is a truism that if you continually exaggerate the faults of the ordinary man and generally try to impress upon him what a very inferior creature he is you will succeed in most cases in making him a debased spiritless thing. On the other hand, if you notice his good qualities, you inspire him to do better. To me the great wonder is not, that Negro criminality is so high, but that it is so low under the great provocation. This becomes all the more remarkable when one considers that the Mexicans, Italian, Russian, French Canadian, and Russian immigrants all have a higher percentage of crimes than Negroes."

"What about rape? next asked the passenger.

"Rape in one form or another has always existed among all peoples."

"I mean the rape of white women by black men."

"I can't see where it is different from any other kind of human rape except that it proves very profitable to the newspapers who under the circumstances can certainly not regret the occurrence, froth as they will."

"Do you mean to say that you see nothing abnormal in this unmentionable crime by black men?"

"It seems to me that there are certain black men who seek out white women in the same manner that certain white men seek out black women. Now since the former cannot get the desired object with anything near the facility that the latter can, they sometimes resort to open attack in the same manner that if a rogue finds he cannot wheedle you out of your money he will get a gun and compel you. This form of rape is peculiar to the United States, and to a very small extent in these parts of South Africa where conditions similar to the Southern States

FROM "SUPERMAN" TO MAN

exist. In Jamaica and Haiti, where black outnumbers white, the white woman is as safe or safer than among her own people. In Cuba, Porto Rico, and in all the South and Central American countries where the black man is outnumbered but where he has liberty of movement this condition is equally unknown. Rape, when its object is a white woman and not mere gratification on the first woman that comes along—is, in short, a reaction of segregation.

"With segregation as the basic factor, here are some of the details that go to make up the Negro attacker of white women: defective mentality; the pictures of nude white women in poses, more or less suggestive, that may be bought or seen in shop-windows; revenge—Negroes see white men making free with many of the prettiest of their women, a type which he, the Negro, cannot sometimes get. He hears, too, the often inflammatory talk by Negroes less ignorant than himself against this and other phases of the color situation; and last, but not least, rum. All of these causes go to make up a lust as paralyzing to the social will as that described by Shakespeare in Sonnet 129, as 'perjured, murderous, bloody, full of blame, savage, rude, cruel, not to trust, past reason hunted, mad in pursuit and possession.' This state of mind, overwhelming a will untempered by refining influences, drives him on to the deed.

"An equally important fact is that the white woman is sometimes to blame. A few months ago a passenger volunteered to me the information of how a white woman, the wife of a farmer, had been caught in bed with a Negro farmhand. The woman, to shield herself, accused the Negro, which you will admit would be a very easy thing to do. When she saw the man burned alive, she confessed."

"But it is usually a low type of Negro that is guilty of this," objected the passenger.

"The greater the reason. In most cases of liaisons between Negroes and white women it is usually the white woman who takes the initiative. Now however bold women may be, they will rarely make advances to any man who is a personality, fearing a refusal, which would be a great blow to their pride. In this case the desire for sexual novelty, overcoming any repugnance to crudeness, they take the man who is not a person-

FROM "SUPERMAN" TO MAN

ality. According to our talk yesterday it must be admitted that many white women, particularly in the South, have a great fondness for Negroes, a taste inherited quite legitimately from their fathers."

"A taste inherited from their fathers!" said the senator to himself in alarm.

Dixon took out his notebook and said: "I have three entries here concerning rape that you might find interesting. Dr. Frances Hoggan, in her address to the Universal Races Congress, says:

" 'In the outlying districts of Africa, where Native life is seen at its crudest, white women have no fear and they pass freely in and out among the Native population, safe and unharmed, never dreaming of danger. It is when natives and low-class white men come in contact with each other that the peril originates, and white women begin to see in the natives a possible source of danger.'

"Dr. Hoggan goes on to animadvert upon the practise of the South African ladies of permitting their manservants to enter their bedrooms while they are in bed or in varying stages of nudity. A missionary in the Church Quarterly Review complains of the same thing. He says that these women will admit their menservants to the most intimate details of their toilettes in the same manner they would 'a dog or a cat'. This condition to no small extent exists on sleeping-cars in America.

"Of those committed to prison for rape in 1932, the whites had 128 cases, and the Negroes 227, which gives a higher percentage to the Negro. But certain foreign-born whites as the Hungarian, Austrian, Italian, had a higher percentage than the Negro. According to the census of 1910, the Italian had 5:9; the Mexican 5.0; and the Negro 3.9 per 100,000 of population respectively, for this crime.

"The Medical Review of Reviews, July 1916, says:

" 'The sexual crimes of the black race against the white are as nothing when compared to the sexual crimes of the white race against the black. Negroes have raped white women retail, but the white has raped the colored women wholesale.'"

"The mortality of the Negro is also greater than that of the white," said the senator.

FROM "SUPERMAN" TO MAN

"This is also due to the Negro's poverty. The rich, while not inherently healthier than the poor, can contrive to live longer and be in better health. That Negroes are more tenacious of life than whites is a well-known fact. According to the census of 1910 there were 2,675 Negro centenarians against 764 white, a proportion of 35 to 1. In 1920, it was Negroes, 2935; whites, 1168, or 25 to 1 in favor of the Negro. In 1930, it was Negroes, 2467; whites, 1180, or 19 to 1. The Negro's higher mortality, like his criminality and illiteracy, may be charged directly against the whites. The attitude of most white men who wrong Negroes, and particularly the women of that group is like that of the adulterous woman mentioned by Solomon who 'eateth and wipeth her mouth and sayeth, I have done nod wickedness.' The feeling—'It is only a nigger' is responsible for an enormous amount of injustice in this nation."

"You were speaking a while ago of that great infidel Ingersoll, what do you think of Christianity and the black man?"

"Now, sir, I appeal to your common sense," replied Dixon. "Consider this—but wait, let me first differentiate between any religious sect that practises the sublime command; "Love thy neighbor as thyself,' and the Christianity of white Gentiles in general, for these Gentiles, though worshipping a Jew, have persecuted the Jews for over fourteen centuries. I have found in my travels that these Gentiles do not like the Jews and the darker races taken collectively; that is, in some parts of the world the Jew is disliked as in all European countries, while there is no antipathy against the Negro. Then in some places as in the United States and South America both Jews and Negroes are disliked. On the whole I have found that the Christianity of the English-speaking Gentile, however devout, when it comes in contact with the darker races in larger numbers, simply does not work. The temptation to exploit them reduces the injunctions of Christ to merest mouthings, as in the Southern States, Australia, India and all Africa. The religion of the Latin races is decidedly more sincere, even in the United States. The Caucasian countries with the lowest degree of prejudice are the Catholic ones, like France, Spain, Italy and all South and Central America.

"Now to speak of Christianity in the United States. Here

FROM "SUPERMAN" TO MAN

is a religion that repeats Sunday after Sunday, year after year, century after century, that the one whose name it bears died to save all men regardless of color—a religion that avers it is a great unifying force. Now here is a people of the same nationality, language, dress, customs, and ideals, and to some extent blood relationship, worshipping this great unifying force, and expecting as a reward to go to the same place; yet because it happens that a certain number of that people are somewhat different in complexion all cannot meet in the same church or even worship in the same neighborhood. And why? For fear of what they call social equality. Can you think of anything more absurdly inconsistent? If they can't harmonize on earth, if they can't live in the same block or work in jobs of equal importance, will they agree in heaven? White God! Colored God, too, eh? Whom does the white American really worship, I ask? The fetish of color, or the Christ whose name he mouths? What material for a satirist! Voltaire nearly laughed the Pope off his throne in the Vatican for less than this. In Florida where white cannot teach black, three white women, nuns, were arrested for endeavoring to instill into Negro children the love of that same God whom the Christians of Florida habitually implore to send light to 'heathens.' For the life of me I can't understand the sort of sentimentality that will weep over Christ lynched nineteen hundred years ago and accept as a matter of course the burning alive of human beings today, even take part in it. Some morbid Negro-haters like Cole Blease are never tired of spouting of Jesus and His love."

"Then you are against Christianity for the black man?"

"If Christianity is that kindliness, courage and courtesy attributed to its Founder in the Bible;—no. The religion of the white Gentile which I have just described;—yes. From what I have seen, and read as occurring, in Africa I know that this sort of Christianity is one of the greatest enemies of the darker peoples and the poor white ones also, and the sooner both see it, the better. I do not mean to disparage the great work by men like Livingstone, Moffat, Dan Crawford, and Father Damien, but I do know that these good men are usually followed by the dishonest Christian trader with his whiskey, diseases and immorality under the pretext of bearing the white man's burden,

FROM "SUPERMAN" TO MAN

which, is only a polite name for loot. The white man must first be humanized, Christianized, if you will. Until that is done the weaker varieties of mankind may expect very little else from his Christianity than the prospect of being plundered. Let the white man, I say, put into practice those Christian principles, he accuses the darker races of not having."

"But," objected the senator, strenuously, "Christianity has done a great deal for the Negro. Look what a solace it was to him in slavery."

"Solace! Solace! did you say? To enslave a man, then dope him to make him content! Do you call THAT a solace? Would you call a chloroform burglar, for instance, a solace? No, that's the work of an arch-devil and a cowardly arch-devil at that. The honest fact is that the greatest hindrance to the progress of the Negro is that same dope that was shot into him during slavery. Many Negro sects, perhaps the majority, never stop to think what they are doing. They have accepted the white man's religion pretty much in the same manner as, if they had remained in Africa, they would have worn his old tin cans, as a charm. As I sometimes watch these people howling and hullaballooing, I cannot but think that any other process, religious or otherwise, would have served just as well as a vehicle for the release of their emotions, and that, so far as Jesus is concerned, any other rose by that name would smell as sweet to them. The same holds true of the poor white mountaineers of Kentucky and Tennessee who are also violently religious and immoral. The slogan of the Negro devotee is: Take the world but give me Jesus, and the white man strikes an eager bargain with him. The religious manifestations of the Negro, as a group, need to be tempered with hygiene, in the same manner that those of the whites need the spirit of Christ."

"Another fact,—there are far too many Negro preachers. Religion is the most fruitful medium for exploiting this already exploited group. As I said, the majority of the sharpers, who among the whites, would go into other fields, go, in this case, to the ministry. In most Northern cities dinky Negro churches are as plentiful as dinky Negro restaurants. Many of these preachers are thorough-going rascals who have discovered a very easy way to get money and to have all the women they want.

FROM "SUPERMAN" TO MAN

Needless to say, they are a great hindrance to those earnest ones really working for the betterment of their people."

"You said you had been in the Near East. What do you think of Mohammedanism and the Negro?"

"From what I saw of it in Egypt, Turkey and other Islam countries I think that while its pretensions are lower than Christianity, it is more humane. Islam is as liberal to its dark-skinned followers as Christianity is illiberal. In fact, every other form of religion is more liberal than Christianity. Ranking next to Mohammed is a Negro, Bilal. Islam knows no other bond but religion. White, black, yellow, brown, it matters not as long as you are of the faith. Christianity—I speak almost entirely of the Anglo-Saxon brand—likes the Negro only when he is content to be a flunky, just so long and no longer. Islam, with all its faults, on the other hand, inspires him to be a man."

The senator took up his newspaper and resumed his reading. After a while, he asked: "What party do you think Negroes ought to vote for?"

"I do not think that Negroes ought to give their votes to any one party. Since they are American citizens they ought to vote for all the parties, seeing that none of them has the monopoly of right. Moreover, all these parties, however divided in creed, have fundamentally the same ideas regarding him. Are not these parties made up of the individuals that discriminate against him singly? The Republican party is regarded as our traditional friend, and most of our progress has been attributed to its efforts on our behalf. I think however that such progress as there is, is due to our own energy, to our being in the most prosperous of all countries, and to aid from individual whites, rather than to the Republicans. I have always considered the Republican party responsible for the greater part of the hardships we have suffered in that it did not make some practical provision to aid the freedmen in gaining economic independence. The Republican party actually does more harm than good to the masses of the Negroes from what I know of its methods in Negro wards. A few Negroes get positions, but it is usually at the moral expense of the others. Gambling-joints are, or used to be, openly permitted. Although this party makes a great show of love for the Negro around election time, agitating the color question

FROM "SUPERMAN" TO MAN

most fearfully, it would gladly get rid of him if it could in order to flirt with the white South. The Republican party, in this respect is like a man allied with a woman he considers below him and whose company he barely tolerates. Seeing another woman he much prefers, but who will have nothing to do with him while his connection with the other woman holds, he would gladly get rid of the old love, but dares not break away, fearing the harm she could do him.

"Of course, since 1936 there has been some change in the Negro vote, and some of what I said applied largely to years preceding that. But they are likely to be again just as I said because politics in America see-saws between the two major parties."

The senator seemed much pleased, "That's very, very sensible," he said. "It's the same thing I have always said myself. The Negro gives his votes to the Republican party as if he were still voting for Lincoln. All that is necessary is to mention Lincoln's name to them. They remind me of a flock of sheep. If sheep are coming from a pen and the first ones have to jump over a bar in doing so, all the others will make the same jump though the bar be taken away. Abraham Lincoln has been taken away; his successors are no more like him than vinegar is like honey, yet Negroes continue to jump Republican in a manner that makes me think they believe Lincoln is still alive and running for President."

"And what about the Democratic party?" he asked a little later with some hesitation.

Dixon out of deference for what he considered must be the political creed of the other, hesitated, but finally decided to give his frank opinion.

"A more characteristic title for the so-called Democratic party would be Negrophobic party. Its attitude to us is just the opposite of what its name signifies. (Of course there are broadminded men in both these parties.) It is also necessary to distinguish between the Democratic party South and the Democratic party in certain Northern municipalities, like New York, Boston and Portland, Me. In many parts of the South this so-called Democratic party is spectacular. It would appear that the successful candidate is he who can abuse the Negro and spout

FROM "SUPERMAN" TO MAN

most vociferously about white domination. The Negro, inconsequential as these politicians make him out to be, is the dominating
factor of their lives. Despite their airs of contempt they live
chiefly for him and after a lifetime of brooding on him, they
themselves, have unconsciously become all that they imagine
him to be. Some of these men even if they have a sense of
justice can never exercise it; they must act with the mob if they
want to keep their jobs. Take the late Senator Watson, when
he was head of the Populist party. Had he but declared a stand
for all citizens regardless of color, it would have meant his
political death. Weininger's statement that the politician is a
prostitute, is at least true of a good many of this type.

"And the result of this policy is an abundant display of verbal
pyrotechnics to please the crowd. Take men like Heflin and
Vardaman. Their sole function in Congress was that of a fire-
cracker—to entertain simply by making a noise. And, of course,
the louder the noise the greater the applause of the child-minds.
This type of Southern politician has raved so long about the
Negro to the exclusion of everything else, that according to the
law of cause and effect that part of his brain connected with the
Negro must be hypertrophied from overuse, while all the rest
is atrophied from disuse. I seriously believe that if the Negro
were suddenly to be removed from the South these great statesmen would be so out of place that, like victims of amnesia, they
would have to begin life again as infants. But in spite of this,
the so-called Democratic party in the South possesses one ad-
mirable trait, that the Republican party hasn't—that trait is
frankness of expression. It declares itself a white man's party.
It does not want the Negro and says so."

"What do you think of the Communists and the Negro?
asked the senator.

"The Communists," said Dixon, "did a splendid social service
not only for Negroes, but whites as well, between say 1920 and
1936. They were the principal ferrets of injustice against the
working people and the most outspoken. America would
certainly have been worse off but for their activities.

"Nevertheless, I do not like their tactics. They are oppor-
tunistic to the last degree, and are quite as nasty in their way
as the vested interests, whom they condemn, are in theirs. The

FROM "SUPERMAN" TO MAN

Communist aim, so far as I can see, is to create chaos in this nation, and during the confusion seize the government. In Russia, they have proved just as murderous and blood-thirsty as the worst of the Czars. If ever they came to power in America, I'd head for the wilds of Γ ιzil, because judging by the talk of some of them, they'd be the greatest head-chopping off concern you ever saw.

"Furthermore, I find them too materialistic. They talk too much about the belly and the boss. Man does not live by bread alone. I have been in parts of the world where people got all the food they wanted with a minimum of effort, and I found life, at times, excruciatingly boresome. The Communists would destroy, if they could, much of the finest in life, because they deem it capitalist propaganda. I think the truly civilized man is interested in preserving all the records of the past, whether it be church art, capitalist art, communist art, or what not. Some of my finest moments of esthetic pleasure have been spent in the old churches and cathedrals of Europe. I detest propaganda, and since I am more interested in life as a whole, I find the Communist fare arid, and almost as tiring as the theologic dope.

"As regards the Negro, the Communists, as I have said, are outspoken, and have done very much in publicizing the evils from which he suffers. I know Communists, who, I believe, are as sincere in their efforts to obtain justice for the Negro as were the abolitionists. Yes, I also know Catholics, Republicans, and Democrats, who are just as active and as sincere as this type of Communist. But such people are not the party, any more than similar people are the Republican party or the Democratic party. The Communist party, as I said, is highly opportunist. Now what proof have we that if ever the Communist party finds the Negro a handicap, instead of a spring-board, that he will not toss him to the lions? How do we know that he won't be like that white man who will start a business in a Negro neighborhood and when he gets on his feet, move to the more profitable white neighborhood and bar Negroes?

"Furthermore, there are Communists who were trained in Negrophobia in their youth. Some try to suppress this, but it sleeps very lightly, and will not need much arousing. I notice, also, that while Communists get into quite a lather about the Negro proletariat and the share-cropper, the Negro, who is already fairly well-off, does not appeal so much to them. Indeed, he is often regarded as an exploiter. This leads me to believe that if the majority of Negroes got up in the world, the Communists wouldn't be quite so friendly to them.

"One fact more: Communism, as I have seen it, is largely a matter of the emotions, by which I mean that when the Communist gets a change of heart, he often becomes the most rabid anti-Communist, just as Catholics sometimes become bitter anti-Catholics. It is said that a very thin line divides love from hate; and an equally thin one divides Communism from Fascism in spirit. I am judging by actions and not by what the Communist constitution says. America has a constitution too; but what does it mean to the majority of our most ardent patriots?"

"One thing, I'm certain," said the senator. "They ought to be outlawed."

"Permit me to disagree, sir. Every individual and every group ought to be free to express their opinions and to hold office, if they proceed according to constitutional methods. The Communists came into being as the result of certain economic injustices, and if you suppress them you are just going to create a similar group under another name, that's all. I know of but one agitator, said Lord Napier, and that is injustice. Let the moneyed, and the would-be moneyed, people, of this nation be less grasping, and the Communists will be as harmless as a toothless wolf. Again, sir, if you suppressed the Communists, what would certain of our big industrialists do for a bogey? I am convinced that most of what is called Communism in America existed as far back as the Declaration of Independence."

"Perhaps you are right about this," said the senator, "but returning to the matter of the Negro vote, you will admit the necessity and wisdom of barring black men from the polls in parts of the South where they outnumber the whites. The white man is better fitted to govern and he will give the colored a far better government than the colored can give him. We do не want a return to the horrors of Reconstruction."

FROM "SUPERMAN" TO MAN

"Colored! White! A difference of so much paint. Does paint vote? That the honest and intelligent citizen and he alone should have a voice in the government of any country is so evident that it is unnecessary for me to say so. Why the effort to bar all Negroes, good and bad, and not unfit white men? I'll tell you, because political tricksters find it very much easier to corral the vote of the whites by an appeal to race hate.

"With regard to a return to the horrors of Reconstruction, this would be impossible but for the revival of the Ku Klux Klan. There are no post-war conditions; no carpet-baggers; the Southern whites are more educated and less resentful about the Civil War; and the Negro is fourteen times more literate now than then. I have no doubt that in every Southern community you will find Negroes possessing all the educational qualifications of the average white Southern aspirant for office."

The senator considered the newspaper in his hand and asked, "What do you think of the press and the Negro?"

"The press," said Dixon, "especially the large dailies, has undergone such a great change in its attitude toward the Negro since about 1920, that I find it hard to believe. Back before the war, agitation against the Negro was prominently featured. Some yellow journal was the instigator of nearly every race riot and lynching. Today, it seems to me that the Negro press does more in displaying Negro crime than the white press.

"However, there is still some subtle anti-Negro propaganda even in certain of the large dailies. And here and there in the South are still some openly vicious white newspapers. Let any unfavorable thing happen, in which Negroes are involved, and they will puff it out greatly. Such remind me of what Schopenhauer said about newspaper men and the way they create alarm. 'Herein,' he said, 'they are like little dogs; if anything stirs, they immediately set up a shrill bark.'

"We can but hope that this general change in the press has come to stay—that it will not shift back as did the French press under the Hitler strain in 1940."

"But aren't you forgetting the influence of books such as 'The Freckled Jeopard'?" asked the senator.

"Since writers like these make their appeal directly to the color vanity of the unthinking and usually incompetent whites.

they do a great deal of harm. Any man who sets out to tell one group of humanity, however worthless it be, that it is better than any other group has an easy and lucrative task.

"And the men who do so are rascals pure and simple. Their sole aim is to fatten on the ignorance of others. I refer especially to Thomas Vixon, who according to a leading historian, is the most misleading of those who write against the Negro. According to Vixon, one drop of Negro blood damns its possessor mentally. Vixon, too, is a Southerner, and as I said, unmixed Caucasian descent in the South, must be conceded; it can rarely be proved. While his motion picture, 'The Abortion of a Nation,' was showing in Chicago, it happened that a Negro was accused of attacking a white woman, and the alleged incident was used to advertise the play with a full page ad and lurid type. Vixon's plays have caused several riots and lynchings. This man is the most mischievous of the many literary sharpers that prey on the emotions of the novel-reading public.

"There are many points of resemblance between the prostitute and this type of literary man. They use intellect and motherhood, those highest gifts that Omnipotence gives to man and woman, respectively, not as a means of blessing humanity, but to blight it; these authors make a living by catering to the lowest of the mental vices—prejudice; the prostitute by catering to the lowest human passion—lust. The prostitute's aim is to make money, though in doing so, she strengthens mankind's greatest enemy—disease; their aim is also to make money though they strengthen the twin-brother of that enemy—Ignorance. The prostitute, the counterfeiter, the vendor of diseased meat, the boot-legger, and the Thomas Vixon type of author are the greatest perverters of society that I know of. I am looking forward to the time when the average reader of novels will have enough self-respect not to surrender his emotions to the will of men of this low type."

The senator did not reply. Dixon continued:

"But is is only non-thinking whites who allow themselves to be thus swindled. The arguments of these writers, scientific and sentimental, are so padded with rhetoric, so childishly exclamatory and exaggerated that were it not for hysteria these non-thinkers could not but see through the cheat, so transparent

FROM "SUPERMAN" TO MAN

is it . One of the heartiest laughs I've ever had was after reading
one of the Negrophobe books. Honestly, I pitied the man who
had to carry around such thoughts of his fellowmen. This book
is to be found in most of the leading libraries of the country.
In the copy in the Chicago library I saw all sorts of annotations
mostly against the author. This one on page 124 interested me,
(I have it here in my notebook): 'If you think I believe what
you print, you are a fool. I was born in Chicago and have a
colored teacher and several colored friends. You don't know
colored people of the North, you fool—written by a white boy
14½ years old.' "

"I read the book through twice and it reminded me strongly
of a filter whose function is to let the good escape and retain
all the impurities. And in this instance as the filter was an
animated one it deposited its own mud. I found the book a
most interesting study, not of the Negro, but of the author—
Robert Wilson Shufeldt. Later when I saw the man himself I
was not surprised. He possessed one of the surliest faces I have
ever seen on a human being—just like a dog getting ready to
bite. Even Thomas Vixon with his wild-eyed, neurotic way
can see something good in Negroes but to Shufeldt everything
about them is as tasty as a green persimmon. This man, it
appears to me, hates humanity, and himself most of all, and uses
the Negro as a vent for his bile. He tells with great gusto how
he had Negro boys to commit self-abuse for twenty-five cents;
and uses this instance to prove the depravity of Negroes!

"Dr. Robinson of the Medical Review of Reviews says that
there is a shameful chapter in the history of American medicine
entitled 'The Negro.' I am sure that Shufeldt must be the chief
contributor to that chapter. Circe, with her magic wand used
to transform men into the kind of animal whose nature they
suggested—lions, tigers, jackals, as the case might be. The
companions of Ulysses, as you will recall, were turned into hogs.
Had she espied this scribbler it is difficult to conceive how he
could have escaped the incarnation of a scavenger-buzzard. Although Shufeldt's book is so interesting a study of his putrid
soul, I object to its presence in a library in company with the
works of Havelock Ellis, Loeb, and Fabre. In most of the leading
libraries even innocuous sex-books are kept from the general

FROM "SUPERMAN" TO MAN

public while here is a dirty sex-book open to youths. The proper place for such a book is in a museum of literary monstrosities for the use of sociologists.

"To my mind there are three points held in common by these authors; first, they invariably begin by declaring their sympathy for the Negro, whom they then lambast with a vindictiveness that makes me wonder how they would ever be able to express themselves had they declared themselves enemies; second, the kink in their vision; and third, the great preponderance of their emotions over their intelligence. As a rule they evince all that lack of reasoning power they attribute to Negroes. The hysterical preacher in Thomas Vixon's 'Freckled Jeopard' has his exact counterpart in a Negro "prophet" I knew who won considerable fame by stirring race hate. Thinking citizens will laugh at men of this type—never take them seriously. I speak against them merely because I see how they are adding to the already large sum of human misery."

"But some of these men are sincere—they are really expressing their honest opinion," said the senator.

"For that matter," replied Dixon, "so are burglars and hold-up men expressing their honest opinion of private property when they stick a gun in your ribs. Some of these men are, as you say, sincere, but for that matter, cannot a half-wit be quite as sincere as the wisest man? There is Professor William B. Smith of Tulane University, who has written a book to prove that the Negro is not a human being. Is Professor Smith more sincere than the Dowieites of Zion City, Ill., who used to maintain that the world is flat and has four corners like a table?"

Dixon took out his notebook and said: "Lest you might think I am exaggerating I will give you a sample of the logic of these Negrophobists. This is from Shufeldt: 'Black wenches,' he says, 'are constantly sought by white men of the various planes of society for carnal gratification.' He goes on to say that the far greater part of the intermixing has been caused by immoral white men, and then further on as a remedy against amalgamation, he advocates the emasculation of Negroes."

"Here's another jewel of humor from the same writer, "He speaks of mulattoes; he says:

FROM "SUPERMAN" TO MAN

" 'Some are wonderfully handsome creatures, with superb figures but handsome and fine-physiqued only in the sense that our American skunk is likewise a beautiful creature. It is only a black animal with more or less of a white stripe in it that is given to stealing chickens, and can when irritated elevate its tail and raise the most outrageous stink, which is quite sufficient to check the progress of any Anglo-Saxon, however robust and civilized he may be,'

"Here is something yet more humorous. This was uttered in the hall of the so-called greatest deliberative body in the world by one of the illustrious type of statesmen, the South usually sends to represent her. Says this verbal pyrotechnist:

" 'Go down to the Pension Office, and take out those sons of the cocoa-nut region who sit there with big brown drops of sweat coming out of their foreheads. Kick them out' Turn this brood of African tree-climbers out to earn a living on the farms and in the fields.' "

The senator laughed heartily.

"But is is to the whites that these stupid men of letters are doing the most harm," continued Dixon, "their mission, so they say, is to uphold white supremacy. They, however, could find no surer way of shattering it. If the color jingoes of America, Australia, and South Africa had the ability of seeing beyond their own noses, they would see that the great effect of their writings is to excite the darker races against the whites and to increase hatred for the whites all over the world. When the average white person reads one of these diatribes against darker humanity its effect is to make him push his chest out a little more; but when a non-white reads it, it stirs him a thousand times more powerfully to push that chest in. All the darker races are at the stage where an insult to one is an insult to all. And don't forget that the darker races outnumber the whites four to one. If this sort of thing keeps on, the day will surely come when white men will find as much difficulty in travelling in certain countries as the Chinese and the Japanese have in the United States and Canada today. The whites are building a ring of exclusion around themselves that may later be used by their enemies to hem them in. The ancient Jews did that, and when they weakened their enemies said, "You built a wall around yourselves because you thought yourselves better than anybody else; now you stay in there.' No man or group of men can afford to insult others gratuitously; they are mortal. Being so they must weaken some day.

"The present generation of whites is making the biggest mistake of its life and storing up vials of wrath to be poured on the heads of their children. I am no prophet but I have the ordinary vision to see that the unjust and the oppressor, however much they may thrive for a while, are sure to come to grief in the long run. This is a law of life and operates as relentlessly as all the others. If this sort of thing keeps up generations of the near future will curse the present one even as those of Civil War days must have cursed the introducers of slavery. 'It is impossible to build up an empire on force,' said Napoleon, and he ought to know."

"I had never looked at it in that light before," admitted the senator.

"I'll tell you an incident, unpleasant though it is," continued Dixon, "just to show you the effect of one of these anti-Negro productions on a Negro—an almost typical case.

"A friend of mine—usually rational—confessed to me his feelings about a picture that was going the rounds. He said that when he saw this picture, defaming his people and noted how the white audience, persons of apparently the best class, were wrought to the highest pitch of enthusiasm over it, a supreme hatred for all white persons came to him, and that he was praying to God that one of them would but touch him and thus give him a chance to brain the offender. To make it all worse, he said, they had the audacity to sing, 'My Country, 'tis of Thee, Sweet Land of Liberty.' Similarly, a white woman told me of how she took her little boy to see the picture and she said that when he saw the Negro attacking the white woman, (as it is in the picture) he said he felt as if he could kill every Negro. I know nothing about the art of government but I do have common sense enough to know that agitation of this sort would never be tolerated in a country whose lawmakers knew the first rudiments of that art."

"Regrettable as this is, what are you going to do about it?" said the senator. "This is a free country."

"Free country! Free mischief! Ought people to be free to stir up race riots? Riots that kill citizens and destroy property

FROM "SUPERMAN" TO MAN

as at Tulsa and East St. Louis?" He added: "Men like Byrnes, Cotton-Ed Smith, and others who are always yapping at Negroes would do well to shift their attentions to the vices of their own people—yes, let them look into their own hearts and they will see: 'It is the old story of the dog barking at his own shadow. It is himself that he sees and not another dog as he fancies.' "

"Well," said the senator, "there are many persons who have befriended the Negro."

"I have been thinking of them. I have always maintained that there are two kinds of citizens exactly alike: those whites who say all Negroes are bad and those Negroes who say all white persons are. One group is merely the racial counterpart of the other. Many white persons have been benefactors of the Negro, even in the teeth of jeers and ostracism from their own people, as certain Northerners who have given up promising careers and gone South to devote their lives to training him. There are also those, (South as well as North) who, through press and pulpit, have striven and are striving to get justice for him. Others, again, have given most generously of their means. Men and women like these, as were Voltaire, Victor Hugo, Elizabeth Frey and Harriet Beecher Stowe, are the conscience of their generation. Such persons are the living, embodiments of the great American ideal—that ideal which declares that all men are born free and equal."

"But I must not forget to mention that friends of the Negro may be divided into three classes: those who believe in segregated justice, this type predominates in the South; those who stand for equal justice only because it offends their sense of the fitness of things, but who have a dislike for Negroes, particularly full-blooded ones, this type predominates in the North; and those who really think the Negro is human and should be treated as such, and even among these I have met a few who declared they had a heart-ache at the mere sight of a Jew."

Dixon consulted his watch. He knew he would be at the next station before long and that as this was the last night he would probably not have a chance to talk to the senator again, so he decided to summarize his arguments. He said, "Looking back on the conversations I have had the pleasure of having with you, sir, and supported by a mass of other information,

FROM "SUPERMAN" TO MAN

gathered from the most reliable Caucasian sources as well as based on my own observations, I am firm in the belief that every argument brought forward or that can be brought to prove the inherent inferiority of Negroes, is based on ignorance or prejudice. I am certain that there is no bad trait possessed by the black man or any other color of man, that does not exist in equal proportions among the white, in short, that 'black is not so very black, nor white so very white.' We see also that the so-called Negro is disliked not for his features, or his imputed bad traits, but for the color of his skin and the nature of his hair."

"But is that the real reason," he asked, in a spirit of raillery, "For instance, many of the most prejudiced whites have Negro intimates that they would defend if need be with their lives. Again, if a man, however black, has money he will find millions of whites ready to defer to him. Foreign Negroes, too, or any Negro who can pass off as Spanish, French, Mexican, however dark—in short, anything else but a colored American citizen is better treated. No, it is due neither to color, nor hair, but to a silly unreasoning American custom—a custom so utterly opposed to everything bordering on intelligence that the sheer wonder is that these people never happen to see themselves in their true light and have a hearty laugh at their own expense."

"What do you think would offer a solution to the problem?" asked the senator, seriously.

"A sense of humor."

"Name something easier."

"Then I should like to see the formation of a national commission for an inquiry into the subject—one that didn't merely eat up the taxpayer's money—and thus ascertain the best means for adjusting the relations between these two bodies of our citizens. There are also three methods which I have always thought would help, namely, text-books in the public schools, teaching the true scientific knowledge on this matter of race, making no special reference to the color situation in this country; the establishment of federal schools in these Southern States that cannot or will not give education to all their children, and a Negro adviser or two in the President's Cabinet. I mean outspoken Negroes, and not those picked by politicians, white philanthropists, or white-black radical groups. The matter is

FROM "SUPERMAN" TO MAN

sufficiently serious to be taken in hand by the federal government, and the stoppage of the evil now would—indeed, I know it will—save the future generations a great deal of trouble. Consider what would have been saved to this country if the slaves had been freed at the founding of the Republic—600,000 lives, fifteen billion dollars—and the South would not have been in the decadent state it now is! Man has intelligence. Should he not use it to ward off disaster?

"I do not see why we in the United States with our superior education should be behind all the South and Central American countries in this matter. This country is big enough and rich enough—and broad-minded enough, too, when it will—to admit of every citizen having a square deal, and yet leave a mighty surplus. A little more assertion of our better selves—a little more patience in dealing with others will go a long way toward making us and them happier. Hamlet's injunction to Polonius regarding the players is a most excellent one. When Hamlet, as you may recall, sir, enjoined Polonius to take good care of the players, the latter said: 'My lord, I will use them according to their deserts.' But Hamlet exclaimed:

" 'Ods bodykins, man, much better! Use every man after his deserts, and who shall 'scape whipping? Use them after your own honor and dignity; the less they deserve, the more merit is in your bounty.' "

LAST DAY

"The strongest is never strong enough to be always master; unless he transforms his strength into right and obedience to duty."—J. J. Rousseau.

The next day, before arriving in Los Angeles, the senator, calling Dixon, invited him to sit and with an air of frankness and earnestness that astonished him greatly, said: "I want to thank you for enabling me to see the other side of the story. I never realized until now the great injustice that is being done to certain American citizens, and also the vast amount of ignorance that we white people have to combat in our own people. Hitherto, I have prided myself on my broad humanity: I now see how narrow it was.

"As for myself, I'm too old to change. I was trained from infancy to consider myself better than Negroes, and you can't teach an old dog new tricks. Perhaps I didn't need any training at all, and as you said, if there were no Negroes around, I'd be looking down on other white people less fortunate than myself. But I'm going to do all I can to disseminate the truth, as you have so competently told it. I think every true American should do his best to end this great evil. Yesterday, you spoke of a Negro American, who was a great Shakespearean actor: What is his name? Yes, Ira Aldridge. Now, I have been thinking that since a Negro could win such high dramatic honors, it would be possible to find Negro talent for our best dramas. The connection is this (here he handed Dixon his card): I have interests in a large motion picture studio and I have been thinking that in order to create a better understanding of the Negro I would get Negro actors for such plays as call forth the highest and best expressions. I shall endeavor to have our studio start with a few and hope to popularize the venture. And in the matter of historical romances, I shall instruct our script writers to find out if any of the personages were Negroes, and have Negroes play the roles. I recall we have had several movies from the books of Alexander Dumas, but how many who have seen "The Three Musketeers," or "The Count of Monte Cristo," know the author of those wonderful stories was a Negro? And why not a picture on the life of Dumas himself? We have had Zola and others. In the meantime, you shall hear from me. Call

FROM "SUPERMAN" TO MAN

at our studio at any time within the next few months and I will
show you how we make our pictures."

He extended his hand and Dixon grasped it cordially.

When the train arrived at Los Angeles he lingered after the
other passengers were gone to say good-bye to Dixon.

"I am going to do all I can to make our beloved America a
real republic," he said:

"There's very good reason for hope," said Dixon, "I'm of the
firm opinion that the majority of the white people are not so
much against the Negro as that they don't know. As the French
would say they are *plus bete que mechant.* Color prejudice is
only a result of certain ignorant teachings. The white American
to whom the feeling against the Negro means so much, had he
been born in Europe and remained there, would have had some
other kind of hate or phobia, such as dislike for Germans, or
Frenchmen, or Italians, or Jews, or other white people.

"A century ago both New York and Massachusetts had jim-
crow cars, like the Southern States. Today, the jim-crow car is
not only gone but both these States have laws penalizing color
discrimination. Chattel slavery disappeared in the South; lynching is becoming extinct, too. There is every reason to believe
that the full light of justice will yet dawn even on the South,
if those of us who have the vision will work untiringly
courteously toward that end. Good-bye, sir."

Printed in the USA
CPSIA information can be obtained
at www.ICGtesting.com
LVHW010408250624
783914LV00001B/249

9 781930 097995